Future Teacher

The Ultimate Guide For First Time Teachers

Evelia Moon

© **Copyright 2020 - All rights reserved.**

The content contained within this book may not be reproduced, duplicated or transmitted without direct written permission from the author or the publisher.

Under no circumstances will any blame or legal responsibility be held against the publisher, or author, for any damages, reparation, or monetary loss due to the information contained within this book, either directly or indirectly.

Legal Notice:

This book is copyright protected. It is only for personal use. You cannot amend, distribute, sell, use, quote or paraphrase any part, or the content within this book, without the consent of the author or publisher.

Disclaimer Notice:

Please note the information contained within this document is for educational and entertainment purposes only. All effort has been executed to present accurate, up to date, reliable, complete information. No warranties of any kind are declared or implied. Readers acknowledge that the author is not engaged in the rendering of legal, financial, medical or professional advice. The content within this book has been derived from various sources. Please consult a licensed professional before attempting any techniques outlined in this book.

By reading this document, the reader agrees that under no circumstances is the author responsible for any losses, direct or indirect, that are incurred as a result of the use of the information contained within this document, including, but not limited to, errors, omissions, or inaccuracies.

Table of Contents

INTRODUCTION 1

CHAPTER 1: DAY 1 IS THE MOST IMPORTANT DAY 7

    FIRST IMPRESSIONS ARE IMPORTANT 7
    ESTABLISH A ROUTINE 10
    EXPLORE THE ENVIRONMENT 12
    PREPARING FOR YOUR FIRST DAY 13
    BE ASSERTIVE, BUT FRIENDLY 24

CHAPTER 2: KEEPING YOUR LEARNERS' ATTENTION 27

    DEALING WITH THE 'TROUBLE CHILD' 28
    ATTENTION-GRABBING TACTICS 30
    1. *Set Clear Expectations* 31
    2. *Practice Patience* 32
    3. *Keep the Energy High and the Pace Quick* 33
    4. *Incorporate Physical Movement and Diverse Activity* 35
    5. *Provide Frequent Feedback* 38
    6. *Use the 10:2 Method* 42
    7. *Allow 'Think Time'* 43
    8. *Play Games!* 44
    9. *Strike a Chord* 46
    10. *Use Clever Attention Grabbers* 46
    11. *Do the Unexpected* 47

CHAPTER 3: MAKING EVERYONE FEEL INVOLVED 49

    TEACHING APPROACHES THAT FOSTER A SENSE OF BELONGING 53
    STRATEGIES TO MAKE LEARNERS FEEL VALUED AND IMPORTANT 57
        Introductions Are Important 58
        Get to Know Your Learners 59
        Practice Listening to Your Learners 61

    Prioritize Meaningful Relationships................................. *62*
    Identify Your Learners' Needs and Emotions................... *63*
    Show an Interest in Learners' Lives *64*
    Foster a Sense of Community, Support, and Care in the Classroom *65*
    Be Consistent *67*
    Use a Reward System *68*
  PLANNING FOR AT-RISK LEARNERS 70

CHAPTER 4: HOW TO NAVIGATE THE UNIMAGINABLE..........73

  STRATEGIES FOR DEALING WITH THE UNEXPECTED. 75
    1.   Breathe *75*
    2.   Give the Learners a Chance to Speak..................... *77*
    3.   Address the Behavior, Not the Person *78*
    4.   Avoid the "Blame Game" *82*
    5.   Always Aim for a Win-Win Situation...................... *83*
    6.   Set a Goal... *84*
  THE HEART APPROACH 85
    1.   Hear *85*
    2.   Empathize *86*
    3.   Assess... *87*
    4.   Refer... *88*
    5.   Tell.. *88*
  HOW TO RESPOND TO INAPPROPRIATE BEHAVIOR 89
  ALWAYS REMAIN CALM AND COURTEOUS...................................... 92
  COMMUNITY IS IMPORTANT!.. 96

CHAPTER 5: ONLINE TEACHING AND 'THE NEW NORMAL'....99

  UNDERSTANDING TECHNOLOGY 101
  LET GO OF PERFECTIONISM 104
  CONSIDER LEARNERS' EQUITY OF ACCESS.................................... 105
  SET CLEAR EXPECTATIONS.. 107
  THINK BEFORE YOU WRITE 108
  VIDEO CONTENT GOES A LONG WAY 110
  CREATE A SOCIAL MEDIA COMMUNITY.. 111
  KEEP THE CREATIVITY FLOWING 114
    1.   Creative Boosts *114*
    2.   Creative Constraints... *115*

  3. Creative Sparks..*117*
LET THE LEARNERS DO THE WORK 119
A GREAT TEACHER IS A GREAT TEACHER 122

CHAPTER 6: MANAGING YOUR TIME LIKE A BOSS 125

BE STRATEGIC WITH YOUR PLANNING 126
START AND END WITH A PURPOSE 128
BE AWARE OF CHALLENGES BEFORE THEY ARISE 129
  1. Designing Lessons and Assessments....................*129*
  2. Socializing at Work...*130*
  3. Nonessential Materials..*131*
  4. Parent and Learner Meetings.............................*132*
  5. After-School Help..*133*
  6. Plan for Potential Crises......................................*134*
PROCRASTINATION IS POISON 135
PLAN REALISTICALLY 137
HIDE WHEN YOU CAN 139
CREATE A SUPPORTIVE COMMUNITY 139
LEARN TO SAY NO! 141

CONCLUSION 143

REFERENCES 147

Introduction

Take a moment to picture your first day as a teacher. You have spent all night trying to decide how you would introduce yourself to the learners and what you would say. You've considered whether you want to be the cool teacher or the strict teacher. You're not sure whether you want to be the crazy and creative teacher or serious and grown-up. You've considered opening with a joke, but you've seen too many films where the audience doesn't react. Besides, they might think you're too eager to please. You've gone through thousands of cliché icebreakers and ideal motivational speeches. You've even considered doing an impression of Robin Williams in *Dead Poets Society*. Finally, you resolve to take it as it comes. You will simply try to be yourself and build a relationship with the learners. You resolve to introduce yourself, allow the learners to do the same, and take the rest as it comes. You may have come across a creative icebreaker and you feel confident that it will get the learners talking.

The day finally arrives. You sit anxiously through the staff meeting and jump up as soon as the bell rings. You greet your learners as they enter the class and then another teacher walks in. Confused, you ask the teacher what is going on and find out that you are in the wrong classroom! Embarrassed, you apologize to the teacher and ask for directions to your own classroom. By the time you find your class you feel lost, embarrassed, and stressed out. Nothing went as planned and all your preparations have been rendered mute. You know what they say, the best laid plans of mice and men often go awry.

Rick Smith once said, "Being a new teacher is like trying to fly an airplane while building it."

This quote has definitely hit the nail on the head! Being a new teacher can be daunting, challenging, and frustrating. Months, even years, of planning, imagining, and idealizing has left new teachers with an idea of teaching that is idealistic and often very unrealistic. The fact of the matter is, being a teacher almost always defies expectation and teaching youths rarely goes as planned. There are countless aspects to consider and an unlimited amount of factors to account for. It can be difficult to maintain the image you have created in your head and be the teacher you've always imagined yourself to be, whilst having to deal with all the unexpected factors and surprises that come with being a teacher. Fear not, these are challenges that every teacher has had to face at some time. If you ask any teacher, I'm sure they can share a few hard lessons they had to learn during their first year of teaching. They will likely tell you that each hiccup and setback has been worth it. You are, after all, changing the world one learner at a time.

By purchasing this book, you have taken the initial step to becoming the best teacher that you can be and overcoming that daunting first year of teaching. This book is an easy-to-navigate user manual for new teachers and will show you all you need to know about your first year of teaching. It is not only useful for new teachers, however. This book is a resource that will prove useful for any teacher that aims to improve themselves and be the best teacher they can be. Once you have finished this book, you will feel confident with the information you have gained to be successful in the world of teaching. You will be able to take any situation head-on and will even be able to navigate those seemingly impossible situations that come up from time to time.

This book gives you a thorough breakdown of useful tips you need to know and consider during your first year of teaching. It will provide you with the tools you will need to successfully thrive on your first day and steer your way through your first year. I will show you all that you need for making a memorable first impression on your learners and colleagues and how to maintain that impression. Another useful element which the book incorporates is a number of effective tips to keep your learners' attention in the classroom and keep them interested for the long run. Furthermore, I will equip you with a plethora of actionable strategies for making sure that all your learners feel important and appreciated. This will invariably improve their academic performance and behavior in the classroom. Disaster will inevitably strike, and this book will provide you with plenty of tips, tricks, and strategies to minimize the damage of these situations and take them as they come. The book will also help you to deal with the new technological demands that have surfaced so rapidly over the past century. It will show you how to deal with online teaching and how to keep your head above water in the so-called "new normal." Not only that, but it will equip you to create the best and most conducive online environment for you and your learners. Finally, and very importantly, this book will show you how you can manage your time more efficiently and effectively without risking burnout. By managing your time effectively, you will be able to focus on what is important and rid yourself of unnecessary distractions and disruptions. These factors are, essentially, the cornerstone of what it means to be a good teacher. By informing yourself on how to navigate these factors, you will be able to navigate the teaching profession with ease and enthusiasm.

My name is Evelia Moon. I have been a middle and high school teacher for almost 20 years. I have taught in three different states across America. I am passionate about teaching and I love being around and working with kids. I have a special knack for relating to kids and getting along with them. Aside from teaching, I have been studying child psychology for the past 12 years. It is important to me to help you become a teacher who can seamlessly navigate the complex world of young people. I have seen too many wonderful human beings get swallowed up by the endless drama and chaos of adolescent youths. This book has been one of my passion projects in conjunction with my passion and skill as a writer. I have written this book to pass on my wisdom and experience to as many worthy people as possible. In doing so, I hope to help and inspire many teachers to become the best teacher that they can be. Ill-informed and unequipped teachers can wreak havoc on a child's life and development. This is why this book has been so important to me, and I hope you will find it useful, informative, and inspirational.

If you are a first time teacher, then this book is certainly for you. If you have spent years trying to envision the kind of teacher you want to be, this book will make your vision possible and attainable. If you are passionate about being an inspirational and life-changing influence on the lives of young people, this book will show you how to create a caring and conducive environment that will inspire personal, academic, and emotional growth in your learners. You will learn how to be a supportive presence in learners' lives, whilst still maintaining a life of your own outside of teaching. It is true that teaching consumes you and soon becomes your reality. It is still possible, however, to be a great teacher whilst having your own personal life. If you wish to find out how you can become a life-changing and inspiring teacher, even in the most restrictive and extenuating circumstances then, by all means, dive in!

Chapter 1:

Day 1 is the Most Important Day

If you are a teacher, then the first day of the school year is the most important day. If you are a new teacher, then your first day of teaching is equally important, whether you start at the beginning of the year or later in the year. Your first day and your initial interactions set the tone for the rest of the school year. You know what they say about first impressions—they last, and you will never get a second chance at a first impression.

First Impressions Are Important

Consider these words by Anthony St. Maarten for a moment: "Your energy is always your first impression. It is the foremost perception others will have of you. This initial energy introduction is a calling card you cannot fake."

First impressions are a powerful thing. They often affect how someone will view you for a long time, and changing these impressions aren't easy. It is therefore important to create a strong and lasting first impression that will have the learners excited to have you as their teacher. First impressions give learners an idea of your boundaries and limitations, or the lack thereof. First impressions are very important to learners when they decide whether they can take chances with you and how far they will be able to manipulate you. It is therefore important that learners know the truth about you from the get-go. Establish your boundaries on the first day, so learners know where they stand with you. Show learners the truth about who you are, what you expect, and how much you are willing to take. This will set the tone for all future interactions with your learners.

First impressions are not only important for your learners, but also with your co-workers. The first day can often be intimidating, especially when you are surrounded by older and more experienced teachers. Teachers tend to form cliques and group themselves when they get together, and fitting in might not be easy. Your sense of importance may not be very high on your first day, but it is important to make sure that your co-workers are aware of your presence and the space you intend to take up in the school. Unfortunately, as with all places of work, the 'new guy' is often considered easy to manipulate, and your co-workers might confuse your 'newness' with lack of experience. As much as you have never taught in your own classroom, you should be prepared and be aware that you have a right to take up space in the school. You have studied and worked very hard for the chance to be a teacher, and you deserve the space you have been given in the school. Let your self-confidence communicate this for you.

Susan C. Young (2017) offers the following advice: "Building self-confidence is like building a muscle. Your confidence grows in response to your intensity of usage and the level of performance you require from it. If you don't use it, you may lose it. Stretch, flex and build." You may not feel confident on your first day, but as they say—fake it 'till you make it. Displaying confidence is important if you want to be taken seriously.

Remember that you will need your energy to last, so don't use it all on the first day. As much as the first day is important and you want first impressions to be memorable, you will need to carry that energy with you through the school year. You don't want to start off with a bang and be unable to maintain that level of energy. Doing so will affect your teaching at a later stage in the year. Make sure that you are able to maintain the same level of energy and enthusiasm that you present on your first day.

Establish a Routine

What you do in the morning and how you spend your mornings can affect your whole day. If you spend the morning running around to get things done, chances are your day will be chaotic. Try to view each morning as a new opportunity and be deliberate about the way you plan your mornings. Make sure that you have ample time to accomplish what you need to, and make provision for those slow mornings where nothing seems to go according to plan. Try to spare at least 30 minutes to relax and enjoy your cup of coffee. This can be far more effective and calming than sleeping for an extra 30 minutes.

Before you go to school, try to maintain your usual routines. A sudden change in the way you normally operate can throw you off and might affect your functioning during the day. Try to get up at the same time you normally do and stick to the same morning routine by doing the same activities you normally do in the morning. If your current routine is more directed toward a holiday situation, try to establish a routine at least one week prior to make sure that your body isn't shocked by the sudden change. Try to maintain an evening routine as well. Evening routines have been proven to improve sleep quality, and you will be able to fall asleep faster if you have a set routine. Getting enough sleep and feeling refreshed in the morning is important for optimal functioning, and your learners need you to be on your A-game in the classroom. Of course there will be days when you don't feel rested or you haven't slept well. This is a part of being human. Having a routine will help reduce these days and ensure that you are able to function as well as possible, as far as possible.

Routines are not only important for you as a teacher, but establishing a class routine is also very important. Setting a routine helps the learners to stay focused and keeps them from being easily disrupted. Learners who are disrupted too much tend to act out, and you want to avoid that from happening as far as humanly possible. Besides that, establishing routines in the classroom can save a lot of time. If learners already know what tasks to accomplish, and how to execute these tasks, they will be able to do them much more quickly and efficiently. This will save you a great amount of time and energy and save the lesson from a lot of disruption and distractions. By establishing a classroom routine, you will also spend less time explaining to the learners how to go about completing certain tasks.

You don't need to have the same routine every day. This will indefinitely bore the learners, and they will become distracted anyway. You might try implementing a different routine for each day of the week or planning your lessons according to a number of pre-set routines. Spend the first day, or even the first week, teaching the learners these routines and ingraining how these routines work. Soon, learners should be able to implement them effectively, and your lessons should run like a well oiled machine.

Explore the Environment

Be sure to arrive early on your first day. Being early not only looks professional, but it will provide you with enough time to get acquainted with the environment and familiarize yourself with your surroundings. You will have more than enough time to set yourself up, prepare yourself, and recap everything you want to do or say in your lessons. Once you have arrived at the school, make time to acquaint yourself with the surroundings. Walk around the school and familiarize yourself with the terrain. Make sure you know where everything is and take note of the places you might need to access later on. Do this without a map, if possible. This will allow you some time and space to get a little lost and explore the school more freely. You will also learn more about the school than you would if you relied on a map. You might discover different spaces and locations you would not have paid attention to had you seen them on the school map.

While you are getting acquainted with your environment, take a few moments to introduce yourself to the faculty, the learners, and anyone else you meet along the way. This is a good way to help you feel more at ease and settled in your new environment. You will be able to present yourself more authentically without feeling too nervous or stressed. Introducing yourself before the day starts will also help you make some allies before the madness begins.

Something very important is not being afraid to ask questions. Asking questions is a good way to get to know your surroundings and to understand the inner workings of the school. Make sure you know who to approach when you need specific information or you need access to something. This will also help you to determine where and how you can solve any problems that may arise. You will know who to ask regarding certain situations or queries. Ask questions about the school's procedures so that you know them. This will help you feel more confident in your own knowledge and will leave you feeling more at ease in the environment. Knowing the school's procedures will help you to already feel more part of the environment, and will conserve you a lot of time and keep you from errors at a later stage.

You might try keeping a running list of questions that you have sorted into two categories: questions you need answered now, and questions that can wait until later. Jot these questions down as they come up to keep yourself from forgetting to ask them. Whenever you have an opportunity to ask a question, you will know which questions you need to ask.

Preparing for Your First Day

One mistake that most teachers make is over-preparing. Although it is important to be prepared, you don't want to be over-prepared. Not only does over-preparing create more work for you, but it will make unexpected interruptions more difficult to deal with. If you have a rigid schedule or plan in mind, it does not allow much room for unplanned changes or unexpected events that may arise. Remember that no one is watching you that closely and no one will care if you've done extra on your first day. Over-planning and over-preparing will only lead to burnout early on in the year.

Burnout involves experiencing chronic stress that will eventually lead to a variety of other factors, including cynicism, detachment, and exhaustion. Burnout can affect your sleeping pattern and quality of sleep. It can also lead to forgetfulness, trouble concentrating, and depression and anxiety. It can even affect your weight or appetite. It is therefore important that you prevent burnout as far as possible, since this will affect your ability to teach effectively.

Start by aiming to have everyone on the same page by the end of the first week. Once you have moved past the first week, you can take stock of everything that you have accomplished or failed to accomplish. Based on these revelations, you can now begin to plan more effectively.

Here is a list of preparation tips that will help you to be prepared enough without being overly stressed or overworked on your first day already. These tips have been suggested by 3P Learning (Ankucic, 2020) and will definitely help you to be more prepared for the first day of school.

1. Build excitement.

Introduce yourself in a way that is creative and exciting. Using an introductory video or bringing flyers or brochures that share fun facts about you are just some ideas on how you can introduce yourself in a way that is fun, exciting, and creative. You can even play a question and answer game where the learners can ask questions about you. Try to share some aspects about yourself that are relatable. Remember that you want the learners to connect with you.

2. Send a welcome email to the parents and learners before the first day of school.

Introducing yourself before the first day helps ease the learners' anxiety, especially if they are starting at a new school. It will also put the parents at ease to know that their child's teacher is open and enthusiastic about their role as teacher. Parents often feel more confident and at ease with their child's schooling if they know the teacher. In your welcome email, you may wish to include some facts about yourself, information on how to reach you, and supplies that learners will need to bring to school. You may also want to add some fun content to the email, such as pictures or videos of yourself or ones that reflect something of your personality. This will make the learners feel more at ease for the first day, and it might help them to feel more excited about being part of your class.

3. Decorate your classroom.

Decorated learning spaces can encourage learning and creativity and will help learners to feel a sense of belonging. Not only that, but with the amount of time you and your learners spend in the classroom, making it a bit more 'homey' and inviting can't hurt. Don't make it too busy, however, as this may distract the learners during lessons and may hinder the learning process. Avoid overloading your learners' senses, as this could become a barrier to their learning. Keep the decorations simple, but fun. You want your classroom decorations to be engaging and motivational, not distracting. Some tips to consider is displaying learners' work, depending on the age group you are teaching, or displaying inspiring role models. This can include pictures or quotes by inspirational figures to give learners something to aspire to. Avoid cluttering your classroom with too many decorations, as this will make your classroom seem disorganized. Try to balance your wall colors. Instead of keeping all your walls the same color, consider having one bright wall and painting the other walls with muted colors.

Make sure that your decorations match the kind of environment you are hoping to create. Inspirational quotes or posters, or even a thematic approach, can be effective and will likely get learners excited about being in the classroom. You may even consider involving the learners in the decorating process to make your classroom feel more like home. Helping to decorate the classroom will also help learners to feel more proud of their classroom and take ownership of the classroom space. It also contributes to the sense of community in your classroom.

Remember to allow space for natural light to stream in. Unless you have a problem with glare or distractions outside, keep your windows uncovered. Natural light helps the learners focus more effectively and may even give them a greater sense of freedom. You don't want your learners to feel trapped in your classroom. If you don't have windows or you need to cover them up for some reason, make sure that the classroom is well-lit. This promotes focus and academic achievement.

   4. Prepare for the meet and greet.

This is another important aspect of preparation. Know what you are looking forward to in the year ahead. Have a clear statement prepared on how you will communicate with the parents. This is an important thing to consider and will put parents at ease, since they are often concerned about their children's education. Ask parents and learners questions that will help them to feel involved and included. Using icebreakers is a great way to introduce people and lighten the atmosphere.

Introduce the parents to your classroom and explain how you are planning to conduct your classroom. Tell the parents what you expect from the learners, and tell parents what they can expect from you. Share your expectations in terms of homework and assignments, so parents can make sure that their children are keeping up with their classwork. You may even wish to share your grading protocols and policies, including the steps that learners can follow if they aren't happy with their marks. This will prevent outraged parents from barging into your classroom to fight with you at a later stage. Informing the parents on your grievance procedure can save both you and the parents a lot of time and effort. Inform the parents of your contact details and office hours so they know where and when to reach you.

Don't be afraid to show your personality. You want parents and learners to know who you really are and you definitely want them to see that you truly care about the learners. Showing your personality can be a good thing. It reminds the learners and parents that you are a unique and relatable person.

5. Write down your why.

Washington Irving said that "Great minds have purposes, others have wishes." Having a purpose in teaching is important, as it will drive your entire teaching practice. Every now and again, take the time to reflect on why you became a teacher in the first place. This will help you to evaluate your practice to determine whether you are fulfilling your purpose for becoming a teacher.

Explain your purpose for the year and consider why you are doing what you are doing. This is a good thing to consider because it will impact the way that you will navigate throughout the course of the year. If ever you feel lost or you lose your sense of purpose, you can look back on your why to help you regain your purpose.

Sharing your purpose will also show your learners and parents, even your co-workers, that you have direction for the year and that you chose teaching for a reason. Sharing your purpose will inspire others to have confidence in you and your abilities.

6. Establish rules.

Geoff Petty makes the following statement in a teaching guide: "Experienced teachers don't deal with problems, they prevent them from occurring." In order to prevent problems from occurring, you need to implement a set of rules.

Establishing rules in the classroom is a cardinal factor in preparing for the school year that cannot be overlooked for a number of reasons. Creating a sense of consistency in the classroom is important not only for learners' stability and sense of security, but it will also be significantly useful in classroom management. It is important to establish rules early on so that learners know where the boundaries are and they are aware of what is acceptable. Your class rules should be simple and easy to follow. Try not to create too many rules, as this might complicate things. You can always add more rules later if you feel that the initial ones are not sufficient.

On the first day of school, introduce the most important rules explicitly in a way that is short, sweet, and powerful. Make sure the learners understand the implications of these rules. You may even involve the learners in setting additional rules and determining the consequences for breaking each rule. Doing this will encourage the learners to take responsibility for their learning. Learners are less likely to complain about the consequences if they were set by themselves. Remember, however, that learners can be silly and unreasonable, so make sure that you monitor this process carefully and settle on a list of rules that you and the learners can agree on.

Once you have agreed on a list of rules and consequences, make sure you write them down and display them in the class. You may even print an individual copy for each learner. This will ensure that they can see the rules everyday, and will therefore have no excuse for breaking them.

7. Start setting class goals.

Setting class goals early on in the year will give the learners a sense of purpose. Goal setting is the cornerstone for motivation. It gives the learners a sense of purpose for the learning process and gives them something to strive to. Setting class goals will help you and the learners stay focused on a particular task or desired outcome. It will give you and your class something to work toward and focus on during the lesson, term, or year based on the kind of goals you have set. Setting goals helps measure the progress of both you and your class. Together, you can look back and determine whether you have progressed from where you started and how much closer you have come to achieving your goals. Finally, goals will help you and your class achieve even more. Once learners feel what it is to reach a goal, they will hopefully want to do even better. There is no motivator like a sense of accomplishment.

If ever learners get discouraged, you can refer them back to these goals. Class goals can include yearly goals, daily goals, or even lesson-specific goals. It is important to have both long-term and short-term goals. Your short term goals should be aimed at bringing you closer to your long-term goals. If your long-term goal is to create a classroom community, for example, one of your short-term goals might be to make a new friend. This will bring you one step closer to your long-term goal of creating a classroom community.

The goals that you set need not only be academic. They can also be behavioral goals or goals for personal improvement, such as making a new friend in the class or not having one case of detention in the class that week. When you give the learners a task, activity, or game to take part in during a lesson, introduce the goals of the activity beforehand. If you are doing an ice-breaker, for example, tell the learners that the goal is for them to make new friends. This helps the learners to keep in mind the purpose of the activity, and learners will therefore be more likely to take the activity seriously.

8. Establish your energy.

Setting the tone and energy of the classroom on the very first day gives the learners a glimpse of what they can expect from you and what kind of energy they can expect in your classroom. Learners who are excited and hopeful for the learning experience will likely try harder in your classroom and be more excited for the school year. It is up to you to get learners excited and enthusiastic about being in your classroom. This can be accomplished through the type of energy you create and exude in the classroom.

Show your learners that you are excited to teach them and build relationships with them by being energetic and enthusiastic. No learner wants to feel like they are unwanted or have been forced on an unwilling teacher. Learners are excited and intrigued by energy and enthusiasm. Being energetic will invariably make your classroom more fun and engaging to be in. Take care, however, to be genuine with your energy. Remember that you have to be able to sustain this energy for the entire year. Never pretend to be someone or something that you aren't. It is very hard to keep up a facade over extended periods of time, especially in the midst of the kind of stress and pressure that accompanies the teaching profession.

9. Give your learners something to look forward to.

Give your learners a mystery or a promise of something that they can look forward to for the following day or the year ahead. This helps to keep the learners interested, excited, and engaged. Creating a sense of mystery or hope for something more will make the classroom exciting and will keep the learners from becoming latent or passive in your classroom.

You may choose to give learners a small taste of what is coming by sharing a single image or quote at the end of a lesson. Doing so may even encourage inquiry-learning by inspiring the learners to find out more. It will give learners something to think about and take home, and it will keep them on their toes.

Take a deep breath and take it slowly. First impressions are important, and your first day definitely is too, but it is not the end if something goes wrong. Remember, teaching is more of a long walk or a marathon than a sprint. Stamina and perseverance is more important than speed. Although it can be beneficial to get ahead early on in the race, there are plenty of opportunities to catch up. As they say—slow and steady wins the race.

Trying to plan too much too early will lead to burnout and a loss of enthusiasm and energy. By moving slowly and allowing space for things to happen as they will, you are helping yourself to feel more natural and composed. The learners will appreciate it more if you are positively patient and collected. Trying to control too many things at once will leave you feeling helpless should something happen to disrupt your plans. While you are trying to make a good first impression, keeping within your comfort zone will help you to get settled more easily. Once you are comfortable and settled, then you can experiment and try new things in the classroom. Let the learners get to know each other and you, first. Find out what makes you comfortable in the classroom and what interests the learners. Focus on setting routines during the first week so that your learners will feel safer and more independent. This will also allow more time to focus on teaching and learning during the rest of the year.

Once you are settled and all these important aspects have been established, then you can change things up. Try not to change too many things at once, however, as this may disrupt the learning process and classroom flow. Introduce changes little by little and make sure that you are considering learners' reactions and input on these new changes.

Be Assertive, but Friendly

While being calm and patient is important, you still need to be assertive. Remember that you are the teacher, the authority figure in the classroom, and you are ultimately in control. It is important to make sure the learners know this truly and unequivocally. Being assertive means being able to stand your ground and you can get your point across without offending or attacking others. People who are assertive can communicate clearly, whilst respecting the rights and disposition of others. Assertiveness is therefore about taking control without needing to dominate or intimidate.

Don't be too assertive or controlling, as this might be considered hostile or even fake, but make sure the learners know that you are the authority in the classroom. Even though you work at establishing community in your classroom, you have the final say when it comes down to it. This is something useful to keep in mind if something goes wrong or does not go according to plan. The learners don't know what you've planned for the lesson, and they won't know if something goes wrong. You control the events and you determine what happens. Stand boldly within the truth of who you are and where you are.

Remember to be friendly! This is an easy thing to force, even if you are generally closed off or introverted and even if you don't feel friendly. It is important to let people—both co-workers and learners—know that you are approachable during these first few weeks. If you don't work to make the first contact as pleasant and friendly as possible, the possibility arises that positive first contact is never made. Learners need to know that they can approach you with any problems that may arise, and this might be difficult if learners think you are unapproachable. If necessary, fake a smile for the sake of the learners and try to be friendly and approachable at all costs.

Finally, remember to have fun! Remember what it was like for you to go back on the first day of school? Try to make this experience as fun as possible for both you and the learners. This will not only make you feel more relaxed and positive, but it will start off the year on a positive and constructive note.

Chapter 2:

Keeping Your Learners' Attention

Keeping your learners' attention is essential for running a smooth and productive lesson. Trying to keep your learners' attention can be challenging, however, and once you lose their attention it can be very difficult to get them back on track. As difficult as it is to keep the attention of one learner, as a teacher you need to be able to keep the entire class focused on the lesson. Diana Graber (2014) mentions using the mantra, "Teach like your hair's on fire" to remind her of the ever-increasing demands of teaching and the importance of maintaining learners' attention and interest.

Twenty-first century teachers have so many things to consider while they are attempting to teach. There is an increasing need to adapt to various different learning styles, keep up with and incorporate technology into lessons, and adjust to the new collaborative trend. Learners have changed significantly, and teachers need to change along with them.

Dealing With the 'Trouble Child'

You will always have those learners who are easily engaged and pay attention to your lessons. Unfortunately, every class also has those learners who would rather not be in your classroom. It is important for you to accept this reality early on. This is a fact and it does not reflect on you or your teaching abilities. You will inevitably have those learners in your class whom everyone is tempted to label the "trouble child." Teachers spend their breaks complaining about these kids and their eyes widen when they see their names—a so-called "teacher's nightmare."

Instead of taking these learners' behavior personally, as you may be tempted, consider these instances as a challenge and an opportunity to showcase your skills as a teacher. This will help you to still maintain the rest of the class' attention. If you allow yourself to get overwhelmed and flustered by a learner's behavior, the rest of the class will see this and will take it as a sign of weakness. Remember that it is your class and you are ultimately the authority. Remind the learners of this fact by taking charge. You can accomplish this by having a list of pre-determined plans and tactics that you can rely on. Establish this list early on, before you experience these instances, to make sure that you are prepared to take charge. Make sure that you have a classroom management plan that will help you deal with difficult situations.

Michael Linsin (n.d.) suggests seven general rules for dealing with difficult learners. Firstly, don't question the learner. Teachers often demand an explanation for learners' behavior and demand a response to force the learner's respect. Doing so, however, will only cause the learner to resent you, and resentment often leads to worsened behavior. The second rule involves not arguing with the learner. Arguing with learners brings you down to their level and transforms you into their equal. This will often result in a situation of hearsay. It will also cause other learners to lose their respect for you. You may have heard of the saying, "Don't stoop to their level." This is a wise piece of advice to keep in mind. Don't lecture, scold, or yell at the learner. This will cause all the learners to not like you and can be very damaging and humiliating to a learner. It also creates a heat-of-the-moment situation where you might say something that you will indefinitely regret.

Rule number four: Don't give learners false praise. Teachers tend to praise difficult learners for merely doing the minimal amount of work. While you might think this to be constructive, these learners will see that you treat them differently. Rather, focus on giving meaningful feedback based on true accomplishments. Remember to be consistent in how you treat learners, even the difficult ones. The fifth rule states that a teacher should never hold a grudge. Try to start each day with a clean slate for all learners. This may be difficult with repeat offenders, but keeping a grudge will only increase tensions and make the learner resent you even more. Don't lose your temper. This may be difficult for some, but once learners see that they can get under your skin, it will happen again. Other than that, when you lose your temper learners lose respect for you or your likeability drops. Finally, do not ignore misbehavior. Ignoring misbehavior will not make it go away, nor will it make the learner behave better. Always enforce the rules, even the small and seemingly mindless ones. It may not seem very important in the moment, but remember that consistency is key to effective classroom management.

Remember that you are in it to change lives and inspire learners, and so-called "trouble learners" are no exception. Keep in mind why you chose this profession in the first place. Ultimately, you want to build a trusting and meaningful relationship with your learners—all of them. Never lose sight of that.

Attention-Grabbing Tactics

It can be difficult to deal with disruptions in the classroom, especially if you are a new and inexperienced teacher. There are a number of tactics that will definitely help you to grab the learners' attention and direct it back to where it should be. Implementing these tactics will not only help you to recapture the learners' attention after they have been distracted, but it will also help you to prevent them from losing interest in the first place.

1. Set Clear Expectations

Before you start, clearly communicate your expectations with the learners. Tell the learners what you will expect of them throughout the year. When you plan activities or lessons, express your instructions clearly, specifically, and in a way that is easy to understand. Communicating your expectations clearly is crucial to maintaining your learners' attention as the year progresses. Not only that, but it will ensure that the learners are aware of the lesson objectives and expectations at all times.

Clearly discuss the expected outcome of an activity with your learners. If you are planning an ice breaker, for example, tell the learners that the purpose is to make friends. If you require learners to finish an activity or discussion within a particular amount of time, inform the learners of this time limit beforehand. Narrate your countdown to ensure that learners know how much time they have left. This also creates a sense of suspense and urgency, which makes the lesson more exciting. Once you have finished the countdown, the learners will have had enough time to finish their activities and discussions before moving on.

2. Practice Patience

Patience is an underrated tactic when it comes to classroom management. If your learners are distracted or disruptive, wait for your learners to calm down and refocus. Learners will inevitably notice your silence and settle down. This tactic will reflect to the learners the importance of paying attention to you during the lesson. This tactic may not be effective for all learners, however, and may lead to even more disruption in some cases. This is why it is important to know your learners and their preferences. If you know that your learners do not respond to silence, there are many other tactics that can be used to refocus learners' attention.

There are always those learners that are easily distracted or fiddle often. Getting annoyed or impatient with these learners will not prove effective or helpful. Instead of getting annoyed or impatient and yelling at them for fiddling, try giving them a piece of playdough to fiddle with while you teach. This is a noiseless and effective solution to ensure that learners pay attention and do not fiddle in such a way that it distracts the others in the class. It will also take away the irritation you may experience while teaching. It is important, however, to make sure that the learner pays attention to the lesson while they are fiddling. If not, you will need to consider another, less distracting alternative.

Remember that not all learners learn in the same way. It might seem like these learners aren't paying attention, but that does not mean that this is true. Make sure to take note of learners' responses or homework activities. This will be a good indication of whether they are, in fact, paying attention during the lesson.

3. Keep the Energy High and the Pace Quick

You have probably noticed that today's children have ever-shortening attention spans. The amount of effort it takes to maintain children's attention is increasing drastically, and there is an ever-increasing demand on teachers to perform in the classroom. This is a fact that teachers have to face on a daily basis; yet, the curriculum is becoming ever-more demanding and cramped. It is therefore important that you meet learners at their own level and strive to teach in such a way that they will want to focus and pay attention to whatever you are teaching.

Don't conduct your lessons with slow, traditional forms of instruction, like the so-called 'talk-and-chalk' method. Keep your instruction dynamic and brisk to encourage learners to engage more effectively. Combine short bursts of information with fun, engaging, and critical activities. Use creative teaching methods and aids that will make your content more interesting and engaging. This will also energize the learners and help them to maintain interest. Enthusiasm is infectious, and if you conduct your lessons in a way that is dynamic and interesting, learners are sure to show more interest and excitement.

You may even start the lesson with a quick jam session to your learners' favorite song to get the learners excited and enthusiastic. This tactic can also be used during the lesson as needed. If you are not a singer, you may consider simply speaking in a different accent or imitating a celebrity just for fun. This is a good way to grab the learners' attention and interest the learners in the lesson in a way that keeps them focused on what you are saying.

Wearing bright and colorful clothing will also help to draw the learners' attention to you and focus on your teaching. This will likely make you seem more interesting and fun. There is a reason that color is used creatively in advertising and marketing, and there is no reason why you can't do the same. Bright colors have been proven to attract attention, which is why wearing bright clothing might prove an effective strategy for attracting learners' attention.

4. Incorporate Physical Movement and Diverse Activity

Stillness will often insight boredom and distraction within the learners. It is therefore important to incorporate some movement or physical activity into the lesson to help learners maintain focus and interest and help them to engage more effectively. Movement and physical activity helps learners to develop better bodies and better minds. Moving around can be both mentally stimulating, as well as physically and mentally refreshing for learners.

For younger learners, you may wish to use puppets or stuffed animals in your lesson to gain and maintain the learners' attention. With little ones, this often makes them more interested and engaged in what you are saying. Having learners act out a skit or help you perform an illustration is another way to involve them in the lesson whilst incorporating physical activity.

You can incorporate movement in small and undisruptive ways, such as asking learners to stand up when they want to ask or answer a question, or having them write their responses or demonstrate a problem on the whiteboard. You can also involve learners in parts of the lesson, such as taking the dustbin around the class or handing out notes. Ask learners to volunteer for these instances or call on certain learners.

Make sure, however, that you involve all the learners and do not merely call the same learners every time. If you work on a voluntary basis, reassure learners that they will have a chance. Ask repeat volunteers to give other learners a chance as well. These small actions can help your learners to maintain their focus during a lesson and minimize distractions.

In order to involve all the learners in the lesson simultaneously, have the whole class respond to a question by writing a response on a whiteboard, or simply giving a thumbs up or thumbs down in response to your question. This is a good way to determine where the learners are and to ensure that some learners don't fall behind. If you have a question with multiple options, or you want to ask learners whether they agree or disagree, you can ask learners to stand for certain options. If you are asking learners a yes or no question, for example, you can ask learners who answer yes to stand up, then ask the others to stand. This way you will be able to ensure participation and you can easily call on learners to validate their responses.

There are, however, also a number of more radical and engaging tactics that can be useful. Having learners switch desks can be a good tactic to get them active and moving. Provide them with a 10-second countdown to find a desk on the opposite end from their current position. This provides the learners with a different perspective and wakes them up. An alternative activity is to tell the learners to switch their position on their seat. Have the learners swing their chair around and sit facing the back rest or with the backrest on their side.

You may even allow the learners an opportunity to sit on their desks. This allows the learners some freedom in the classroom, which may help them to be more enthusiastic about learning. It is fun, engaging, and keeps the learners alert. Taking 10 seconds to move around also provides the learners with a short break and allows them to stretch their legs. It also prevents the learning environment from becoming too rigid and strict. Remember, however, that each learner is different, and these activities might be completely disruptive to some learners.

Incorporating physical movement is not only effective when applied to the learners' role in the classroom. Wandering around the class as you teach can also prove very effective. As you walk around the classroom, learners will likely feel compelled to keep track of your movements and will therefore remain alert. They will likely keep their eyes on you as you move about the classroom, thus ensuring their full attention. You can also easily keep track of learners who are distracted in this way. A simple gesture such as going to stand next to these learners can prove very effective in recapturing their attention. Learners will also feel compelled to pay attention in fear of being identified.

5. Provide Frequent Feedback

Providing feedback is an integral part of learning and assessment. Feedback is an effective way to keep the learners on their toes. It helps them to determine their problem areas or areas of improvement. Feedback also reminds the learners that they have not yet mastered the content and that they still have some learning to do. This will inspire learners to pay attention and rectify their mistakes. Feedback can be harmful if not done correctly, however. Make sure that you provide constructive feedback, rather than destructive criticism. Constructive and positive feedback should motivate learners and inspire success. It is not intended to demotivate or break down learners' confidence. Through helpful and insightful feedback, learners should be empowered to move forward, try harder, and do better.

Ross Crockett (2016) offers seven helpful keys to providing helpful and constructive feedback.

The first important point he raises is that learners should always feel safe. Learners yearn to feel safe and protected, and your class should be an environment where learners feel encouraged to do well and succeed at whatever they may attempt. Some learners can be very hard on themselves due to external expectations from parents, teachers, their peers, and society. Feedback can therefore easily become a negative and discouraging experience for them. It is important that you therefore provide comfort and reassurance, rather than judgement and criticism. Take note of the way you phrase your feedback as well as the tone you take when providing feedback. This can be a determining factor in whether the learners feel criticized or supported.

Another important factor to consider when providing feedback is to stress the importance of teamwork. Let the learners know that you are all working together as a class and as a team. It might also be a good idea to pair learners up so they can help one another. Remind the learners that their peers are there to help them and encourage them to work together. Also remind them that you are available for additional support and help. This will ensure that the learners do not feel alone on their learning journey.

Thirdly, use proactive language when you provide feedback. It is important to be constructive and encouraging. Focus on the positive and let the learners know what can be done about their situation. Teachers need to rethink how they talk to learners about what needs improvement. It is important to highlight both the positive and negative aspects of the learners' work and to always remain optimistic so the learners feel that you still have faith in their abilities. Instead of focusing too heavily on what was bad and what went wrong, provide them with possible ways forward and speak in such a way that you cultivate hope and encouragement rather than instilling a sense of doom.

Crockett suggests that teachers avoid the use of 'should,' 'but,' and 'however' as much as possible. The word 'should' can have psychological effects on the listener similar to that of being punished. It can easily be mistaken as some form of comparison or an unattainable standard of some sort. Using the word 'should' can be very destructive and limiting to a learner's performance. Try to focus rather on what the learner can achieve instead of what they 'should' achieve, as this gives them the sense that you are focusing on their abilities rather than your own expectations and standards. Using the words 'but' and 'however' can also be very destructive and have negative psychological effects. These words tend to cancel out everything that you have said before them. Consider this example: "You are brilliant, but you fail to demonstrate this in your answers." If you tell a child this, they will completely forget the first part of that sentence. Using these words too often incites a lack of self-confidence and creates feelings of inferiority.

Another important aspect of feedback is to ask the learners guiding questions. Learners often hesitate to answer in fear of giving an incorrect answer. Being told that your answer is wrong can be debilitating and humiliating. Reassure your learners that answers aren't inherently right or wrong, and try to reinforce this in the way you respond to learners' answers. The focus of feedback is meant to be on the learner and is meant to be exploratory. Asking guiding questions can be very useful for encouraging problem-solving and brainstorming, and it promotes higher order thinking.

These kinds of questions can also give you a good indication of where the learners are at in terms of their knowledge and understanding, where they get stuck, and what they find interesting about the topic. Asking guiding questions such as "What do you think?" or "Is there another way to approach this?" can invite both reflective thinking and engagement. It also teaches the learners to think independently and critically. While you are asking these questions, pay attention to non-verbal cues to the effects of these questions such as nodding, frowning, or fidgeting. This might also give you an idea of where the learners are at and whether they even understand what you are asking.

Try to use visuals when you provide feedback. In today's digital age, learners are more likely to engage effectively in feedback and retain what is being said when it is presented visually. According to Wayback Machine (3M, 2000), presenting information visually can increase comprehension by up to 400%. They also highlight that humans process visuals 60,000 times faster than text and the average person only remembers about 50% of what they hear. It is therefore an effective idea to use diagrams, images, and sketches while presenting feedback to the learners. This will ensure that learners can understand and remember what you have told them.

Finally, check the learners' understanding. After you have delivered feedback, it is important to check whether the learners have understood all you have said and if any clarification is required. Ask the learners if what you have said makes sense, if they have any questions, and whether they are seeing possible ways to move forward. This will ensure that learners understand the feedback and are able to act on what you have told them. Brainstorming solutions together can also help to build a sense of community and will develop problem solving skills in the learners.

Remember that feedback is not only beneficial and useful for learners, but it can tremendously benefit you as well. Feedback provides teachers with valuable information on the learners' progression, engagement, and understanding of the content. It can be used to inform and improve your teaching. Looking at feedback is a good way to determine where the learners are struggling, to identify common misconceptions, and even to identify underlying issues, such as diagnosing certain learning barriers. You may even find that some learners are lacking essential skills that are important to your subject. Feedback helps you identify these issues and find a way forward.

6. Use the 10:2 Method

This method is very effective for learners who have a short attention span. Try to give the learners about two minutes' processing time for every 10 minutes of teaching. This allows learners to think about what you have said and think of questions or responses if necessary. You don't have to follow the 10:2 ratio exactly. You could, for example, give learners one minute for every five minutes' teaching or four minutes for 20 minutes' teaching. You will get to know your learners soon enough and can adapt your strategies according to their needs and capabilities.

During the two minutes' reflection time, have learners ask questions or discuss with their partners what they have just learned. If you find that silent reflection works best for your learners, you can do that too. This will help them to reinforce their newly acquired knowledge and determine where it fits into their framework of already established knowledge and facts. It will also help you as the teacher determine whether they were able to follow your teaching or not.

7. Allow 'Think Time'

Teachers often teach the content as they planned it, without allowing learners time to think and process what they are hearing. Since teachers know and understand the content so well, they forget that the learners are just learning the content for the first time. They don't always consider that learners might need time to process what they are hearing. Silence is often considered a sign of ignorance or even disobedience. When you ask the learners a question, don't expect an immediate response. Allow the learners at least five to seven seconds to think about the question you have asked, depending on the difficulty and complexity of the question. You may even allow the learners to discuss it with their partners first, before attempting to answer. Some learners take longer to process a question or piece of information than others, so make sure you are not leaving that learner behind. Know your learners, and make sure that your approach allows for all of them to have the best possible learning experience.

You may also randomly and frequently ask learners to repeat what they have said or ask a question about the content. This helps the learners to keep up with the content and keeps the learners focused and on their toes. Asking learners to repeat themselves will also help other learners to process this information. If you want to check whether other learners are paying attention and understanding, you can ask them if they agree or not, and to substantiate their response.

8. *Play Games!*

Gamification is a rapidly growing concept in education. It involves incorporating games into a lesson or turning the lesson into a game. Learners love to play games, no matter how old they are. Incorporating games into your lessons can be fun and engaging, and it will allow the learners to enjoy the lesson a lot more. When you see the learners' focus is drifting during a lesson, give them a mental break by playing a game of *Simon Says* or *I spy*.

You can also play games that are related to the content to help the learners make connections and engage with the content more effectively. Games will likely make the content more interesting as well.

There are a number of games and activities that you can incorporate into the everyday activities that take place in your classroom. These activities will not only make the experience more engaging and fun, but it will make your job much easier in some cases.

When the learners are expected to return to their seats, tell them to imitate a silent animal such as a butterfly or a bee. This will help maintain a quiet and peaceful environment and prevent unnecessary disruptions. It also gives you a lot more teaching time, as there is no need to ask the learners to quiet down. Take note to stay away from sloths and turtles as the learners might take the rest of the period to get back to their seats. These games can be incorporated into the actual learning process as well. You can use a soft ball when learners need to answer questions. Throw the ball to whoever should answer the question. This learner can then throw the ball back to you or to the next learner when they are done. This incorporates games into the lesson and helps the learners engage more with the lesson. It will also help you to choose volunteers and prevent learners from speaking over each other.

9. Strike a Chord

You don't need to use your words in order to regain your learners' attention. Using a fork or a bell to make a noise or turning off the lights can be just as effective at gaining their attention, if not more. A sudden, shrill sound will be sure to grab the learners' attention, and they are sure to turn their focus back to you. Make sure that learners don't have access to these devices, as this is sure to cause chaos in the classroom.

10. Use Clever Attention Grabbers

Use fun and clever attention grabbers such as "hocus pocus everybody focus" to gain the learners' attention. Once the learners hear these lines, they will know that they need to pay attention. Another idea is to use call and response tactics. You may adopt a creative line to which the learners will have a set response. For example, the teacher may say "Alright stop!" to which the learners will respond "Collaborate and listen." This tactic helps the learners to feel involved and will easily grab their attention.

You may also choose a fun word, such as "shazam" or "bazinga." When you say these words, learners will react by hitting the desk twice and then clapping twice, for example. This is a good activity to wake learners up and refocus their attention to the lesson. These tactics will not only create a fun, positive, and engaging environment, but it will also contribute to the sense of community in your classroom and among the learners. It is something they can use to connect with you.

If you notice that learners look sleepy or tired during the course of the lesson, stop teaching altogether. Go to your whiteboard and write a command on the board without saying anything. Continue this exercise with another two or three commands. Make sure that the last command or two is something with sound or definite movement to ensure that learners who haven't caught on have an opportunity to do so.

11. Do the Unexpected

Doing something that learners weren't expecting is sure to grab their attention. This keeps the learners on their toes and keeps them from falling asleep during your lesson. When you see that learners are distracted and they aren't paying attention, do something unexpected and completely random, like dancing or clapping your hands mid-sentence. This will not only recapture the learners' attention, but learners will indefinitely look forward to seeing you. Having a fun and interactive class definitely goes a long way to creating a conducive learning environment and effectively helps ground the learners' attention. Learners love random teachers that are unlike their other teachers. It is refreshing to enter a classroom that isn't strict and boring and where they aren't being yelled at for falling asleep.

You may even choose to tell a joke every now and again. This will surely gain the learners' attention, keep them engaged, and make your lessons more fun—even if they don't find your jokes funny. Learners may even begin to look forward to attending your class. If you are not a joker, you may ask one of the learners to tell a joke.

Teaching outside on a beautiful or warm day will also help the learners to engage better with the content. A change of scenery is good for the learners every now and again, and being outside can improve cognitive function. Fresh air helps to keep the brain awake and functioning properly, and a change of environment can be refreshing. It is important, however, to be aware of your learners' dispossessions and needs, as some learners may be very distracted when they are outside.

Keeping your learners focused and engaged during a lesson can be a challenge. With the right mindset and the right tactics, however, you can easily grasp and maintain their attention. Applying these tactics will not only keep the learners interested, but it will make your classroom environment fun, engaging, and conducive—killing two birds with one stone.

Chapter 3:

Making Everyone Feel Involved

A sense of belonging is one of the most basic human needs. It entails the degree to which someone feels respected, supported, accepted, and valued by those around them. It enables us to see our value in life and helps us to better cope with the challenges that may arise in our lives. A sense of belonging also helps to develop a sense of community, which significantly improves one's experience and sense of importance. A sense of belonging helps us to feel relaxed, receptive, and motivated. It helps learners to develop a desire to do well and achieve more. A sense of belonging and value is core to experiencing academic success.

Learners' sense of belonging is directly linked to their academic performance at school and can have an effect on their behaviour. It affects their attention span and the effectiveness of their learning. It is also linked to their persistence in the classroom and their completion of designated learning activities. If learners feel undervalued or feel like they do not belong, they often tend to let their learning activities or their overall academic performance slip. Learners who experience a low sense of belonging might have trouble seeing the purpose behind their academic achievement and therefore lose their interest in academic activities. A greater sense of belonging among learners significantly improves their level of engagement and affects their academic achievement. Learners who experience a greater sense of belonging in the classroom tend to learn more effectively and often have greater levels of motivation. A low sense of belonging, however, is often associated with delinquent or anti-social behavior, negativity, drug and alcohol abuse, violence, or dropping out of school.

The easiest way in which you can lose a child is for them to feel as though they are unimportant or irrelevant in the bigger scheme of things. Learners need to feel loved and important in order to feel safe and protected in your classroom. It is the responsibility of the teacher to make sure that their classroom is inclusive and supportive. Teachers should ensure that all learners feel important and valued in their classroom, thereby ensuring the wellbeing of their learners. Teachers should plan in such a way that they are able to effectively support learners in the classroom and in the school.

According to research conducted by Education Week (Blad, 2017), 41% of teachers find it difficult to create an environment where learners feel a sense of belonging. They reported finding this especially difficult in light of differences in sexual orientation, gender, race, socio-economic background, and enthnic and disability identities. Learners who come from a bad past or one that is different from the other learners' often find it hard to fit in and therefore tend to become isolated or withdrawn. These learners may even act out in the classroom as a result of their isolation. Furthermore, 80% of teachers consider a sense of belonging important to the learners' experience of success. Forty-nine percent of teachers indicate, however, that they need help to find strategies that will create a sense of belonging in the classroom.

Education Week (Blad, 2017) also notes that learners' sense of belonging tends to decrease once they move to secondary school. There are a number of reasons for this occurrence. This decrease in learners' sense of belonging may be linked to the discrepancy between the learners' prior experiences and their new environment. Learners in secondary school often have a newfound need for autonomy. There is also a drastic change in learners' interactions with their peers and in the type of learning environment that exists. These changes can be difficult to deal with and adapt to, hence the sudden drop in learners' sense of belonging. Furthermore, there is a significant and sudden decrease in the level of support when learners move to secondary school, and teachers tend to offer learners more freedom in certain things. Teachers are not as involved in the learning process and don't necessarily monitor learners as closely. This may create a sense of detachment in some learners. Teachers in secondary school tend to be more controlling and specific in the way they conduct their classrooms. They tend to provide the learners with less autonomy in learning activities conducted in the classroom. Learners are expected to sit still and focus for longer periods of time and their schedule becomes more structured and controlled. The demand on learners also increases significantly, and learners may find this stressful. Finally, learners often need to adapt to bigger classes and more teachers in secondary school. This can be extremely overwhelming and very difficult to deal with. Learners may detach themselves in order to deal with these changes and therefore lose their sense of belonging.

This lack of belonging that learners feel may lead to loneliness, stunted personal growth, and a lack of motivation and independent thinking. A lack of belonging and all problems that ensue may even contribute to delinquent behavior amongst the learners. Diversity among learners often leads to marginalization and separation between the learners, such as the formation of cliques. This is the very thing that teachers need to try and overcome by making all learners feel valued and appreciated and fostering a sense of belonging and community in the classroom.

Teachers are a crucial piece of the puzzle when it pertains to a learner's sense of belonging. If learners consider their learning environment one that is caring and accepting, they will be more likely to adopt the teacher's academic and social values and respond to the teacher's requests. Learners' sense of belonging ultimately influences how they feel about the work they are doing and how much, or how little, they value their learning experience. The level of involvement in your classroom and the extent to which learners feel engaged is ultimately up to you. This may sound like a tall order, but it is your responsibility as the teacher to own it and live up to it. Embrace your place as a role model in the classroom. Learners at school tend to look up to their teachers, whether they want to admit it or not. For the amount of time that learners spend at school, it inevitably becomes their home away from home, and you become their parent away from home. Give the learners something to admire and look up to, and they will more likely listen to you and obey your requests. It is the role of the teacher to foster a caring pedagogy and a supportive environment.

Teaching Approaches That Foster a Sense of Belonging

The way that you conduct your lessons, the way that you teach and your teaching philosophy can directly affect whether your learners will experience a sense of belonging in your classroom. A teacher that wishes to foster a sense of belonging in the classroom should foster high-quality relationships with their learners. They should make an active effort to establish relationships with their learners that are real and meaningful and that promote trust. Learners who do not trust their teachers are less likely to feel at home in their classroom, and the most effective way to build a learner's trust is to establish a relationship with them.

A supportive and caring environment goes a long way to making sure your learners feel valued and important. Make sure that your classroom is a space where learners feel safe, loved, and appreciated. Turn your classroom into a judgement-free space where learners are encouraged to love, accept, and respect one another at all times. This idea may sound a bit out there, but it is possible. Additionally, offer emotional support to your learners when they need it. Make an effort to show an interest in your learners, their lives and their well-being. Make sure the learners know that you are available and eager to help and support them should they need it.

As a teacher, it is important to always try and understand learners' points of view. It can be difficult to understand or relate to your learners at times, but putting yourself in the proverbial shoes of your learners can go a long way to giving you a better sense of what they are feeling or experiencing. Getting to know your learners will definitely help you to gain a better understanding of their point of view, since you are more likely to understand who they are or where they are coming from.

Create an environment that promotes respect and fair treatment. It is important that you respect your learners and they respect you. Remember that respect is a two-way street. Learners will not respect you if you do not respect them. You should also encourage learners to respect one another. This is an important factor to building trusting and meaningful relationships among learners. Your teaching approach and classroom environment should foster positive relationships among learners and encourage mutual respect. These factors contribute significantly to developing a sense of community, which is very important for learners' personal and social development. It is also essential that you treat learners fairly, making them feel equally valued and appreciated. As a teacher, you cannot have favorites or so-called "teachers' pets." It is your responsibility to treat all learners fairly and to make an active effort to connect and engage with each one of your learners.

Your classroom management strategies can have a powerful impact on the learners' sense of belonging. Ensuring that you enforce positive classroom management practices will contribute significantly toward building a strong sense of community and responsibility in the classroom. Negative and destructive classroom management strategies create a negative classroom environment that can be detrimental to your learners' morale. Your classroom management strategies should be specifically tailored to the needs, preferences, and personalities of your learners in order to be constructively effective. Blanket strategies are rarely applicable to every situation and often require some tweaking and adjustment to be relevant and effective to the learners in your classroom. Make sure that your learners have a say in how their learning takes place. Heeding learners' feedback, comments, and recommendations can go a long way to improving the classroom environment and increasing learners' sense of importance and involvement in the classroom. Ultimately, you are the determining party in deciding what happens in your classroom. You can therefore determine what is good for you and what works in the classroom. It may prove beneficial, however, to listen to and consider learners' perspectives and comments also.

Having a collaborative approach to teaching goes a long way to improving teaching and learning experiences. Work with partners in the community to help meet the learners' needs. Consult your school guidance counsellor or another, more experienced teacher if you feel the need. Never be afraid of asking for assistance or advice, as this will improve your teaching. Relying on the experience of other teachers who have been there longer can go a long way in helping you improve your teaching practices. Leaning on the expertise and experiences of others can prove useful and beneficial and will take much of the strain off of you.

Taking part in extracurricular activities can significantly boost the learners' sense of belonging. Taking part in a group activity of any kind will help the learners to find a group of people that they can connect with and rely on. Individual activities can also promote a sense of belonging by increasing learners' sense of importance to the school as a whole. Not only that, but excelling in any activity can be a confidence boost and will provide the learners with a greater sense of self-importance. Reminding learners that their efforts are a part of the school's greater level of achievement and involvement reminds them that their position is important, no matter how good they are or how well they do in a given activity. Providing rewards based on participation rather than only rewarding achievements can significantly contribute toward creating a cooperative sense of community in the school.

Finally, by promoting high standards and certain behavioral expectations in your classroom and the school, learners can feel proud of the school, and classroom, they are part of. Promoting good behavior and high standards gives the learners a sense that they are a part of something greater and more important. Establishing a good school reputation and high standards will therefore also help to promote a sense of belonging and unity among learners. A sense of pride is a great motivator for achievement, excitement, and participation. It also helps to establish a strong sense of community.

Strategies to Make Learners Feel Valued and Important

There are innumerable strategies and tactics that can be used to make your learners feel more valued and important in the classroom. These are merely a few examples, but should give you a good indication of how to make learners feel like they are valued. Valuing your learners will lead to personal growth and a greater sense of achievement among learners, and will help you to establish positive and meaningful relationships with the learners.

Introductions Are Important

Make introductions immediately before you start teaching and get the year started on the right foot. Introduce yourself to the learners and have them introduce themselves to the class as well. This will already help the learners connect with one another at the start of the year and will begin to break down the barriers created by differences early on in the year. You may wish to use an icebreaker or an interesting question for initial introductions. This will help keep the atmosphere light and relieve some of the pressure that you or the learners may be feeling.

Furthermore, give the learners an idea of what to expect. Tell them what the classroom will be like and how you have attempted to personalize the syllabus. Set standards and communicate these standards with the learners. Tell the learners what they can expect from your teaching discourse. Inform the learners of the language they will be taught in, for example. Discuss the kinds of materials that learners can expect to use and what kinds of activities they will be expected to do and take part in. Knowing what to expect goes a long way to helping learners feel comfortable and safe in your classroom and relieves a lot of the anxiety that they might be feeling. It is also important that you challenge any stereotypes that learners may have internalized about you, your subject, or about learning in general. Challenge these stereotypes by doing something totally different from what they would expect in your classroom and encourage them to leave behind any preconceived ideas they may have developed.

Get to Know Your Learners

Getting to know your learners is essential for conflict management and for building effective and meaningful relationships with the learners. Get to know your learners by learning their names, their likes, and their dislikes. It is very important that you become thoroughly acquainted with your learners as soon as possible. If possible, and if you have access to learners' pictures, you can begin to memorize learners' names before the year even starts. This will give you a head start on the year and help the learners to feel special and important on their very first day already. Pursue a friendship with their learners in order to help them trust you. This will help to ease classroom tensions and may prevent a lot of conflicts and problems at a later stage in the year. Remember, however, that you are their teacher first, and then their friend. If learners trust you, they are more likely to feel comfortable to come to you with their problems. If you feel the need to choose between these two roles, you should choose the role of teacher. This is the most important of your roles.

Get to know your learners' likes, dislikes, preferences, etc. by asking them to write a personal essay or to present a speech about themselves and their interests. You may even ask them to design a poster that describes them. Ice breakers are also a fun, effective strategy to help you get to know your learners and to help them get to know one another. Knowing your learners is essential if you want to really understand them and aim to build effective relationships with them. Connecting with your learners will definitely make your classroom experience more pleasant and rewarding.

Misalignment occurs naturally, so try not to be too hard on yourself when this happens. There is, however, always something that you can do to bring outsiders closer to the group and make them feel involved and included. Always bear this in mind when you are teaching. You will not always automatically connect with all your learners, and building a relationship is easier with some than with others. Remember that, although it is natural to align more with some people than it is with others, you cannot allow this with learners in your class. You have to make an effort to connect and build a relationship with all your learners, even if it is harder to connect with some of them.

Gail Godwin once said that, "Good teaching is ¼ preparation and ¾ theatre." Teaching is a lot like acting, and the classroom is your stage. Teachers cannot afford to allow every single personal hiccup to affect the way they teach. Their job is far too important. It is therefore important that you don the role of teacher the moment you walk into your classroom. When you put on your teaching shoes, you leave your troubles behind and your focus becomes the learner. Learners are able to learn better when they feel loved and understood, and it is your role to make them feel this way. It doesn't matter who your learners are or what they have done, teachers can never, ever afford to give up on their learners.

Practice Listening to Your Learners

Ralph Nichols once stated, "The most basic of all human needs is the need to understand and be understood. The best way to understand people is to listen to them." The same is true of the learners in your classroom. In today's busy society, adults rarely take the time to listen to their children, and this has severe psychological effects on learners' self-esteem and their sense of importance. If you want to understand your learners and be able to connect with them more effectively, listen to the way they speak and the things they speak about. This will tell you more than their actual words ever can. Learners are far more likely to feel important and valued if they are truly heard and listened to. Children often feel devalued or unimportant because they tend to be disregarded or ignored by the adults around them. If you truly want to make a difference in your learners' lives, be sure to take the time to listen to them. Never shrug off a learner if they want to speak to you. If you are busy, make an appointment or give the learner an alternative time to come and see you. This will assure them that you value them and consider their thoughts, ideas, and emotions important.

Use learners' feedback and input to inform your teaching. Learners' feedback can be very useful to improve your teaching approach, to affirm your trusting relationship with the learners, and to assess learners' progress. Feedback is an invaluable tool, even if it comes from the learners. Your learners are far more likely to learn effectively if their concerns are heard and addressed. Teachers often operate with the notion that learners know nothing about the teaching and learning process and are therefore wary of listening to learners' inputs. I'm definitely not suggesting that you yield to learners' every request. I am, however, suggesting that you take the time to listen to learners' inputs and try to understand the logic behind their concerns. This will prove invaluable in helping you create a conducive, productive, and learner-centred environment. Learners are far more likely to learn effectively if their concerns are being heard and addressed. You may even find that some learners are facing challenges you have been completely oblivious to.

Prioritize Meaningful Relationships

It is important that you prioritize high quality and meaningful relationships—both among the learners and between yourself and the learners. Schedule office hours for consultations and notify the learners of these times, or schedule one-on-one sessions with your learners in order to get to know them more effectively. This is a good space in which you can allow the learners to discuss their needs and raise any individual questions they may have about the content, the classroom, or anything else. Making yourself available to the learners will show them that you love and support them. It will inform the learners that they can come to you with their needs and concerns. If you encourage learners to come to you with their questions and concerns, they will be more confident in the content and will likely be more trusting of you and their learning environment. By getting to know your learners, you will also be able to notice when they are not themselves. This will help you to show your care and support, rather than remaining oblivious or uninformed.

Identify Your Learners' Needs and Emotions

As a teacher, it is important that you understand the needs and emotions of your learners individually, not just holistically. Understanding these needs and emotions is not enough, however. You need to be attentive to their needs and emotions in order to maintain an effective and meaningful relationship with them. Remember that girls and boys are different. They communicate differently and experience things differently. You can therefore not expect them to act and react in the same way. Girls are more likely to show emotion and tell you how they feel, whereas boys will likely express themselves in some hidden way. Learn to identify these moments so you can be there for your learners.

Similarly, each person and each learner is also unique. They experience things differently and they will learn differently too. It is important to take note of these differences so that no learner will feel undervalued or unimportant in your classroom. Remember that not all learners learn in the same way. Learners have different learning styles and preferences. Making space to accommodate different learning needs and preferences is important to making your learners feel valued and appreciated. Also remember that some learners are shy or withdrawn. It may take them some time before they are able to speak up and participate confidently in classroom activities. Learn to identify these learners and situations, and try to consider other ways in which these learners can participate effectively and show their understanding. The use of blogs or journals may be useful, for example, or even breaking learners into smaller groups for discussions. This will allow learners who are withdrawn to feel less intimidated and will provide them with a space to speak with confidence.

Show an Interest in Learners' Lives

Very importantly—you need to show a genuine interest in the lives of your learners. It is not necessarily about getting to know every aspect of learners' lives, but rather implementing and reinforcing a pedagogy of care in the classroom. It is about creating an active, learner-centred classroom environment where learning is about the interests of the learners, rather than the interests of the teacher. It is about involving learners in the structuring of experiences and asking their input. It is about helping the learners shape their own learning experiences.

Learners need to understand that they are more than a mere student in your classroom, and that they are an important part of the learning environment. Show an interest in the learners' lives outside of the classroom by asking them questions and really listening to the way they respond. You may even find that you have a hobby or interest in common with some of your learners. This provides you with an opportunity to connect with your learners, which will likely make them feel more safe and secure in your presence. It will also help you to connect more effectively with the learners and find some common ground. Finding common ground is an opportunity to make a real connection with the learners and helps you to be able to support the learners more effectively.

Foster a Sense of Community, Support, and Care in the Classroom

Create a community within your classroom. A sense of community is always important to help you foster meaningful relationships and create a safe environment. Ask the learners to work with one another and have them strive for goals together. Have your learners set short term and long term goals for themselves, and do the same with the entire class. In doing so, you will enable the learners to work together to achieve a common goal, while helping each other achieve their respective individual goals.

You can foster a sense of community by establishing a philosophy of respect and fair treatment in your classroom. Encourage the learners to voice their concerns and opinions confidently. Invite learners to brainstorm the classroom rules with you and help you establish these rules. You may wish to establish a list of basic rules that you consider important, but involving the learners in the rule-making process encourages them to take responsibility for their actions and take ownership of their classroom conduct. Having the learners determine the consequences for the rules will also remove the chances that they will complain about the consequences. They will then have no grounds for claiming that you are being unair, so long as you are consistent in enforcing these rules and consequences.

Create a classroom environment that is supportive and caring. It is important that you as a teacher are able to be vulnerable at times to remind the learners that you, too, are human. Learners need to see that you are a human being who also fails and feels sometimes. This will help the learners relate to you more and not see your expectations as something unattainable or impossible. It is important, however, that you show resilience in the midst of vulnerability. This will show the learners that it is possible to be resilient and push through any challenges that may arise. Take some time to talk about stories of failure and resilience to motivate the learners to do their best and never stop trying. Finally, commend the learners' attempts and comment on their strengths. It is important to highlight learners' strengths, since they are often unable to identify these themselves. This will motivate them and encourage them to work hard and do well. It will likely provide them with a sense of accomplishment and will boost their self-confidence.

Be Consistent

Consistency is key! This saying relates to so many aspects of life and of teaching. Learners tend to judge teachers based on their actions, not their words. It is therefore imperative that you practice consistency in the way you treat learners in order to make them feel equally valued and important in your classroom. Learners need consistency for a safe and stable environment where they feel a sense of belonging and can learn effectively. Inconsistency tends to promote notions of distrust and suspicion, and this is no different in your classroom. In order to encourage learners to trust you, it is therefore important that you be consistent in every aspect of your teaching and in the way you treat learners.

Learners may not always understand why they don't like someone or why they feel distrustful of certain people, but it can happen because they don't understand the other person. It is therefore important that you be someone who learners do not feel confused or uncertain of. Don't be afraid to show the learners who you are and express yourself in a way that is not threatening or confusing. If you are unclear about who you are or consistent by changing the way you operate, the learners will be confused due to your lack of consistency and may lead them to distrust you. A lack of consistency may also be threatening to learners and causes a lot of undue stress, since learners never know what to expect from you.

Use a Reward System

You may try developing a reward system. Learners love rewards, and most kids will work that much harder if a reward is involved. Beware, however, of shifting the central focus of learning to the reward it produces. Use rewards to teach learners the value of the work they are doing, but never let the reward become the sole purpose behind their working. Learners need to learn and understand the value of hard work and of your subject. Make sure that you teach them that in the process of rewarding them.

Know the difference between praise and encouragement, and make sure you use the right one for different purposes. Praise is a value judgement based on the end result of a task or assessment. It would involve stating, for example, that the learner has done an excellent job on their presentation, or has written an exceptional essay. A praise statement therefore comments on the complete task or assignment at the end of the assessment period. The problem with praising learners is that the learners can easily become dependent on your praise if they receive it frequently. They will eventually crave your praise for their work and may even become disappointed or discouraged if your praise becomes less enthusiastic. A learner who has consistently received an "excellent" or "exceptional" review on their work, for example, may be discouraged when you tell them that their work is "good." Even though "good" is a suitable comment to receive on your work, learners may consider it a negative response because they are used to "exceptional" or "excellent" comments. Learners react to small changes and can pick up on these quite easily. Learners who consistently receive an average result will likely feel left out or devalued in your classroom if praise statements are consistently used.

Encouragement, on the other hand, focuses on the learners' inputs and improvements, and acknowledges learners' efforts. A teacher may, for example, comment on the amount of research conducted for an assignment, or the creativity used in the writing of an essay. In this way, you can comment on the learners' strengths and help them feel more valued without needing them to do well holistically. Using encouragement is significantly more effective in boosting learners' self-esteem and self-confidence. It encourages self-assessment and contributes to the development of learners' intrinsic motivation. Intrinsic motivation can be very important in helping the learners perform better and boosting their efforts. Encouragement is more helpful than praise, since it can be used even if the learners fail. It helps the learners to identify their strengths and encourages them to try again. Encouragement can be accomplished by rewarding learners for their efforts and improvements.

Schools often tend to focus only on the top achievers in the system. It is crucial, however, that you include all learners in the reward system. The system's tendency to focus only on top achievers very quickly demotivates the average learner, since they feel that they cannot reach the top tiers. These learners therefore fade into the background and don't reach their full potential. Learners need to be encouraged to improve upon their own achievements, however, to ensure that they remain motivated and enthusiastic about the learning process.

Planning for At-Risk Learners

Teachers and schools need to actively identify and plan for learners who are at risk of facing discrimination and marginalization. Some groups of learners may be at a greater risk of experiencing a lack of belonging, depending on their personal background and previous experiences. It is important to be able to identify these learners early on and to plan strategies proactively that will help these learners feel more included and important. The school should plan and implement strategies to promote a greater sense of belonging among all learners, and especially among at-risk learners. Doing so will inevitably reduce learner drop-out rates and increase learners' overall academic achievement. Teachers should support and encourage learners' emotional, behavioral, and social development. Learners should be commended when they develop in any of these areas and should be encouraged to continue growing and developing in all areas.

In order to promote a greater sense of belonging, school policies should promote respect among learners and teachers for all forms of diversity. Acceptance of, and respect for, differences can significantly improve learners' sense of belonging, especially among the marginalized groups of learners. Learners are often ridiculed or labelled as "weird" or "strange" if they are different from the others. Learners need to be valued for their uniqueness, rather than being discouraged from exploring and showcasing their differences. School policies should therefore be intolerant of discrimination, both from teachers and learners, and should enforce respect and acceptance. This is the first step to promoting an inclusive and supportive environment. School policies should also support and encourage teachers to implement fair classroom practices. This can be improved by training and equipping teachers with the necessary skills and knowledge. If teachers are supported and encouraged, they will be more effectively equipped to create safe classroom spaces and a fair classroom environment for the learners. School policies should also seek to promote parental involvement in the school. The level of parental involvement can contribute tremendously to the school environment and the sense of community. Greater parental involvement will inevitably create a greater social connection between school and home. This will reduce the divide between learners' school and home life, and will help learners to connect more effectively in both domains. Finally, school policies should create and promote a culture of acceptance and tolerance among learners and teachers. Implementing these aspects into the school policy will go a long way toward creating a sense of belonging in the school and in the school classrooms.

Being a teacher can be complicated and multi-varied. There are several aspects to consider simultaneously and various things that you need to focus on at once. It can be difficult and very stressful, but doing this is your superpower—use it. Teachers aren't called superheroes for no reason, and what use is a superhero if they do not use their superpowers? When you are in the classroom, make sure that you are the person everyone knows they can turn to, trust, and confide in. This will ultimately make your classroom a safe, secure, and fun environment to be in. Your learners will develop a greater sense of trust, self-confidence, and belonging all thanks to you.

Chapter 4:

How to Navigate the Unimaginable

The bad news—insane and absurd moments can and will happen while you are teaching. This is inevitable. The good news—you can deal with them effectively if you are prepared. Each classroom and each group of learners has its own potential chaos and its own crazy possibilities that may erupt at any time. By being prepared, however, you can get a headstart on these events or situations. Unfortunately, no matter how prepared you are or how much you have planned, there are always some unforeseeable things that can happen. You are a teacher, not a seer, and you cannot visualize all the possible problems, disasters, or catastrophes that may arise in the classroom. You can, however, prepare yourself for the unimaginable, even without knowing what that might be.

As a teacher, you can allow the potential chaos of unimaginable situations to be something fun and entertaining that you can use to showcase your amazing teaching skills. The alternative is utter panic and hysteria. The first step toward navigating these situations is to accept that they will inevitably come up, whether you want them to or not. You can therefore choose to allow these situations to derail you and disrupt your class completely, or you can view them as a challenge and an opportunity to show learners just how great of a teacher you are. Use these situations to fine-tune your skills and learn new strategies and tactics. By adopting this kind of mindset, even the most daunting and disastrous of situations can become light and manageable.

Remember that the way you react in these impossible situations will determine how your learners see you. If you react by becoming hysterical or resorting to complete panic, you will likely lose learners' respect and admiration. If you choose not to waver in the face of chaos, however, learners will likely grow in their respect and admiration for you. Not only will learners respect you more, but they will likely trust you more after this situation. They are also more likely to do what you request of them. Learners look up to their teachers. You must therefore model the same kind of behavior that you want learners to embody and demonstrate. Do you want your learners to waver and panic in the face of a challenge, or do you want them to see it as an opportunity to learn and showcase their skills? I'd imagine the latter.

The way you conduct yourself in all situations will teach the learners something about how they should react to situations in their life. Effective teachers are able to handle difficult situations with encouragement, dignity, and kind words instead of criticism, anger, and harsh words. The ultimate goal is to help the learners feel good about themselves and their behavior, and this is what you want to reiterate. Address learners in such a way that they would want to change their behavior as something they can be proud of. Forcing unwanted behavioral patterns is never effective, but you can help the learners to want to be better.

Strategies for Dealing With the Unexpected.

1. Breathe

This might sound like a cliché, but there is a reason that people always respond to stress in this way. Taking a breath can be powerful in ways that you cannot imagine. Taking a breath in the heat of the moment gives you some time and space to take a step back and evaluate the situation before reacting rashly and impulsively. Not only that, but pausing to take a breath literally calms down your body. When you take slower, deeper breaths, it slows down your autonomic nervous system and pulls your body out of fight or flight mode. Our bodies are linked to our nervous system, and if your nervous system is in panic mode, the rest of our body manifests the same response. The only way to control your nervous system is by controlling your breathing. If you slow down your breathing, your body will also become calmer. Living in a state of panic and shallow breathing produces tension and anxiety, and it can even cause physical pains and strains. Taking a breath helps to release stress and tension.

Besides the physical effects that breathing has on your body, taking a breath before you choose to respond will help you to avoid rash, impulsive, or angry responses. Reacting in the heat of the moment can be harmful to the learner and will produce long-term effects. By responding in anger, you may hurt the learner unintentionally or say something you will regret for a very long time. Reacting in anger will not only hurt both you and the learner, but you will likely lose the trust and respect of other learners. Rather, take a breath and consider the situation. You do not have to respond immediately. Keep your words kind and constructive at all times to avoid breaking down or permanently damaging your learners. Responding rashly can break down everything you have worked hard to establish in a moment, and you will have to work very hard to restore learners' trust in you.

2. Give the Learners a Chance to Speak

If a learner is being disruptive or is misbehaving, give them a chance to respond. This might be the last thing you want to do, but it can make all the difference in the situation. A teacher's first response to disruptive learners is usually to yell at the learner and refuse to let them say anything. When learners attempt to respond, the teacher often considers this disrespectful and rude. Often the very root of the problem lies in the fact that learners feel unheard or invalidated by the adults, and sometimes even the friends, siblings, and peers in their lives. Learners who are constantly ignored, invalidated, or disregarded tend to act out, since this is the only way that they believe they can express themselves. Learners may therefore merely need a space in which they can express themselves and voice their emotions or experiences. By taking a moment to simply listen to the learner, you may be able to dissolve the entire situation.

Acting out usually occurs as a result of an unmet need. These needs cannot be expressed unless one takes the time to listen to the learner speak. Be an attentive listener as a general rule, not only when conflicts arise. Encourage your learners to talk about their feelings and experiences and to express their needs. Help clarify learners' comments by restating them. For example, you may ask the learner, "Are you saying that…?" Or you can say, "What I understand by your comment is…" This kind of exercise will avoid miscommunication and help the learners feel heard and understood. This will likely help to avoid disruptive situations in the first place.

3. Address the Behavior, Not the Person

When learners act out or disrupt the class, their behavior should be addressed immediately. Ignoring disruptive behaviors will not make the behavior go away, nor will it teach the learner that their behavior is wrong. It is important that learners understand when their behavior is unacceptable, and you should reiterate that fact. When you attempt to address wrongful behavior, however, learners may feel that your problem lies with them and not their behavior. This occurs especially when one particular learner is continually reprimanded for their behavior. It is therefore very important that you make a clear distinction between the learner and their behavior. Make sure that the learner knows it is their behavior you dislike, and not them. Take note of the kind of language you use when reprimanding the behavior, ensuring that you are not directing your comments directly at the learner. Instead of saying, "You are very rude," for example, consider saying, "Your comments are very rude," or "Your choice of language is unacceptable." In this way, you are focusing on the learners' actions and behavior, rather than directing your concerns toward the person themselves. Directing your comments at the learner rather than their behavior can have psychological effects and may even lead to feelings of inferiority or incompetence. By focusing on their behavior, however, you are showing the learner that it is something they can change. Their words and actions may form part of them, but it does not define who they are and can be changed at any time.

Always remain respectful and polite, even in the face of hostility. Never be rude or disrespectful in the way you address a learner or their behavior. The way you act, even in the face of hostility or crisis, affects your image and it affects the way your learners see you. Be consistent in the way you treat learners and in the kind of behavior you allow in your classroom. It can be easy to overlook a transgression when it is committed by one of your most well-behaved or academically-excelling learners. It may even seem like less of an offence if you particularly like a certain learner. If a learner constantly misbehaves, under-achieves, or causes problems, however, even the smallest of transgressions can seem like a problem. It is important, however, that you treat learners the same way at all times and punish them with the same level of punishment or the same consequences. You cannot allow one learner to talk in class and reprimand another for doing so, even if one of them is a repeat offender. Learners will likely consider this a show of favoritism and will likely feel victimized or undervalued. Treating learners equally is pivotal to creating a fair and trusting environment for the learners. It is important to create a space where the learners do not feel like they are constantly targeted, even if it is with good reason.

Avoid labelling learners at all costs. Labeling things and people is a natural instinct, as it helps us with association and identification. Labeling an object is one thing, but labeling learners can be damaging and destructive. Teachers tend to describe learners as good or bad learners, and even refer to some as problem learners or difficult learners. Staffroom discussions that center around certain "difficult" learners can get quite insulting and even downright mean. Labeling learners can be very destructive to their self-image and may even reinforce bad behavior. Children tend to think that if their teacher views them as a bad or difficult learner, then that is how they should act. Learners associate labels with expectations, and will therefore often conform to that label for much of their lives or possibly even the rest of their lives. Labeling also influences the views and expectations of others. If a teacher has heard that a particular learner is trouble before they have taught them, it will taint their judgement and inform their impressions when they interact with that learner. This happens unconsciously, and teachers need to be aware of this. Rather than using words like "bad," "difficult," or "good" to describe learners, use words such as positive, acceptable, disruptive, or unacceptable to describe their behavior. This is more likely to focus their attention on the behavior, rather than linking your criticism to the person. Once learners have been labeled, whether consciously or unconsciously, it can be very difficult to lose that label.

Finally, a useful strategy to consider when directing your attention to the learner's behavior is to focus on recognition. Give the learner recognition for their strengths, commend them on their efforts, and focus on the desirable behavior more than the negative or undesirable aspects of their behavior. This will help you to reinforce the good behavior rather than constantly shifting the focus to the learner's bad behavior or their shortcomings. Not only that, but adopting this tactic will motivate the learner to want to do better and be better. Recognition is always a good motivator, and learners will want to receive recognition.

An important tactic that you can always keep in mind is to try and understand where learners' behavior is coming from. Misbehavior is often a direct result of external disruption in the learners' private life. The learner may be going through some personal difficulties and is acting out as a result. It may also be due to an unfulfilled need in their life. By acting out, they are attempting to communicate that need. Studies also found that attention seeking and learning difficulties are other causes of misbehavior (Yuan & Che, 2012). Understanding these factors and how they contribute to misbehavior can go a long way to helping the learner deal with the roots of their misbehavior. Knowing your learners can help you to identify when a learner is disrupted and will help you address their behavior more effectively. Knowing your learners will help you to make more informed decisions when you address their misbehavior, thus preventing you from causing possible damage to the learner.

4. Avoid the "Blame Game"

When addressing misbehavior, always remain polite and respectful. Despite popular opinion, there is no need to be rude when you are addressing a problem or disruption in the class. Always remain respectful in the way you address your learners. This ensures that they maintain their respect for you also. If you fail to show respect to even one of your learners, you will likely lose the respect of all your learners. Furthermore, avoid playing the "blame game." I'm sure you know how annoying it can be when a first grader accuses a classmate of stealing their pencil or touching their belongings. This is fine for a first grader, but you are an adult, and you definitely do not want to sound like that first-grader. Instead of accusing or blaming the learner, simply address the issue. Give the learner a specific and pointed description of what it is they have done wrong and help them to understand the consequences of their behavior. There's no point in getting into an argument or a shouting match with learners. Remember that you are the adult in the classroom and should act accordingly at all times and in all circumstances.

Never, ever ridicule a learner. You may be tempted to put a particular learner back in their place with a single comment or observation, but this is never a wise decision. It may solve the problem temporarily, but in the long run it will be to your detriment—the detriment of the learner and the detriment of the class. By ridiculing or humiliating a learner you will likely have lost that learner for good. You may likely have lost the respect and admiration of the entire class, or worse, have taught them to ridicule others in the face of confrontation. Not only that, but you run the risk of temporarily damaging a learner and creating a lifelong wound. Express your displeasure at the learner's behavior without criticizing or ridiculing them.

5. Always Aim for a Win-Win Situation

Make the learner aware of what they have done and find a way to draw in their accountability. Insist that the learners should accept responsibility for their behavior. Instead of yelling at them from the get-go, ask them what it is they have done wrong. Sometimes, learners don't consider their actions wrongful or harmful and will therefore gain nothing from a simple scolding session. Scolding at the learner will not achieve anything if they do not know what they have done wrong. Make sure the learner knows what they have done wrong and takes full responsibility for their actions.

Furthermore, try as far as humanly possible to create a win-win situation. Place the emphasis on problem-solving, rather than focusing on the conflict or problem itself. Try to find some form of compromise that will be beneficial for all parties involved, whilst leading to a change in behavior. This will likely help the learners feel more accepting of the solution, and you will also gain something in the process. Instead of a screaming match, you will end up with a civilized agreement and, hopefully, changed behavior.

6. Set a Goal

Setting goals can be helpful in every aspect of one's life. If you find that you are on very bad and strenuous terms with a learner, set a goal for yourself. Improving relationships doesn't happen overnight, and you may need some time to improve your relationship with the learner. If you have identified a learner you are struggling to connect with, or are constantly clashing with, allow yourself about two or three months to improve your relationship with that particular learner. If your relationship with the learner does not improve, you might need to seek the help of a professional such as a psychologist or go for educational testing. Relationships and compatibility with learners are not always in your control, and it is sometimes necessary to seek external assistance.

If you find that you experience a lot of misbehavior in your class, set a goal for reducing these instances. Work collaboratively with your learners to determine what kind of goals to set that will improve their behavior. You may even introduce some incentives to speed up the process. This should be done with caution, however, as incentives might keep learners from seeing the true value in improved behavior. It won't happen overnight, and you will learn over time how to handle these situations wisely and effectively. You will make mistakes and not all your strategies will work. Allow yourself some time to figure things out and try to set goals that will help you to improve in these aspects. Don't be too hard on yourself if things don't improve right away. Try and try again. Something, somewhere is bound to work.

The HEART Approach

The HEART approach is another useful strategy for dealing with and managing difficult situations in the classroom. This is a more structured and organized approach to addressing crises and misbehavior, but can definitely be very useful and informative. If you want a more formal, structured approach to dealing with difficult situations, then this is the way to go.

1. Hear

The first step in this approach is to hear what the learners are saying. Take a moment to listen to their response and consider their input on the situation.

Remember the importance of listening to learners. Learners might have a lot more to say than you think. Taking a moment to listen and hear what they have to say might prove invaluable to both you and the learner. It will help you to deal with the situation maturely and as partners, rather than rivals. It will also prevent you from sounding like a superior and treating learners as inferior to you. This is the first step to establishing healthy communication and creating a positive, constructive community in your classroom, regardless of conflicts that may arise.

2. Empathize

Once you have listened to the learner and considered what they have to say, try to empathize with them. Put yourself in their proverbial shoes and consider what they are experiencing and going through and why they may be acting out. Learners might be having some difficulty in dealing with situations in their personal lives and may be using your classroom as a space where they can work through their emotions and express their frustration. Personal challenges, sudden changes, and feelings of inferiority are all factors that can contribute to learners' misbehavior in the classroom. This is not necessarily a personal issue or attack on you or your teaching style. Rather, it is often because of external factors that learners feel the need to express themselves and their needs in potentially destructive ways. It is therefore important to empathize and try to understand the learners' situation before reacting.

3. *Assess*

You have now listened, considered, and processed what the learner has said. You have taken a moment to empathize with the learner and may even have told the learner that you empathize with them. Now that you have an understanding of what the learner is experiencing, the next step is to assess the learner's needs. Based on the information you have gathered, what do you think are the learner's needs in this particular time? They may simply need someone to listen to them or pay attention to them. Some learners may need additional academic support. Other learners, however, may even need help from an expert, such as a psychologist. Based on the information you have gained, you should be able to determine what the learner needs. If necessary, you may wish to talk to a professional or an older, more experienced teacher at the school. If you are unable to evaluate the situation, speak to these people about the situation without divulging the learner's name or details. They may have some valuable insights or ideas with regards to the nature of the problem.

4. Refer

Once you have identified the learner's needs, you will need to refer them to the appropriate places and authorities. In these situations, you may not be able to effectively help the learner yourself. Your role as a teacher is to support the learner and provide a safe space for the learner, but you cannot fill the learner's every need. If the learner needs professional help, refer them to the necessary places or authorities. They will then be able to take care of the situation in a professional and effective manner. You can still support the learner and make sure they are coping, but your role is not to counsel the learner or provide professional help. You may feel compelled to do so, but you may not have the training required to effectively address the problem as extensively as may be needed.

5. Tell

Finally, and very importantly, it is necessary that you notify the relevant authorities of the events that have taken place. This may be your head of department, your principal or even the school counselor. Make sure that you notify the appropriate authorities and fill in a report on the events that occurred. This way you will have a record of what happened, how it happened, and when it happened. Your school may have their own protocol on how to deal with these situations. Make sure that you have reported or recorded the situation for future reference. This may seem tedious or unnecessary, but it may protect you or the learner somewhere in the future.

How to Respond to Inappropriate Behavior

Dealing with inappropriate behavior can be challenging and downright difficult. You may not always know what to say or how to respond in these situations. The important thing to remember is to never ignore the problem. It may be tempting to pretend like nothing happened or ignore the situation until it goes away, especially if you don't know what to do about the problem. Ignoring the problem will not solve the problem, however, and neither will it make the problem go away. In fact, by ignoring the problem you might just be making things worse for yourself and the learner. Facing the problem head on is the only way to deal with it effectively. If a learner behaves inappropriately in your classroom, arrange a private time in which you can talk to the learner away from their classmates and the pressures of the classroom. This will give the learner an opportunity to tell you how they feel and to voice their opinions on the matter without the social pressure of having their friends close by. You will also be able to address the learner more effectively without fear of humiliating them in front of their peers. Moving the learner out of the environment and away from their peers also gives them an opportunity to be vulnerable without being judged by their peers. When you address a learner in front of their peers, they may continue to act out in an effort to save face. Learners are very concerned with their social image, which is why you need to isolate the learner when you attempt to address the situation.

When you address the learner, always be respectful and supportive. You may not want to be supportive after the behavior they have displayed, but learners are in need of your support regardless. Keeping things supportive and respectful will also help both you and the learner to see the situation clearly. Don't get into an argument with the learner. This will only make things worse and will probably cause even more friction between you and the learner. As I have discussed previously, angry, resentful, and hostile responses are never effective or helpful in difficult situations. Keeping your communication kind and respectful helps you to maintain your dignity and keep intact the learners' respect and trust in you.

Beware of getting caught up in the emotional state of the learner. In the heat of the moment, emotions may be high and you may be compelled to get caught up in the learners' emotional distress. You may feel a surge of compassion and an overwhelming desire to help the learner with their situation, but beware! Learners are often experts at being able to use emotions to manipulate others and, even if the learner is not trying to manipulate the situation, it is not your job to counsel the learner. Remember that you are a teacher, not a counselor or psychologist. You can listen to the learner and offer them your support, but refer the learner to the appropriate person for counseling or psychological help if need be. You are in no position to offer professional advice to a learner unless you are a certified school counselor or practicing psychologist.

Just because you cannot counsel the learner does not mean that you cannot help them or that you should ignore the problem. Ignoring the learner's problem can be harmful and debilitating. Acknowledge the learner's distress and let them know that you understand their position. Don't try to downplay the situation or tell them they are overreacting. This might make things even worse. Ask the learner in what way you can be of assistance. You may try to provide possible options or solutions to the learner or ask them to come up with some of their own. Talk about these options and discuss them thoroughly with the learner. Remember that you are not a psychologist or a school counselor. It is therefore important that you do not label or diagnose anything. Only a professional can do that. You are merely acting in a strictly supportive capacity.

Assess the learner for possible signs of self-harm or self-harm tendencies. These are often a clear sign of distress. If you notice that there are signs of this, refer the learner to a professional. Remember that you cannot help the learner effectively if their problems are more severe. You can only offer your support and offer to listen to the learner. You may even offer to walk the learner to the school counselor as moral support. Although this may feel like giving up on the learner or "ratting out" the learner to an expert, referring them to the right channels is ultimately the only thing that will truly help them deal with their emotional distress.

Being supportive and compassionate goes a long way to making a learner feel loved, valued, and supported. Inappropriate behavior often occurs due to deeper issues, and it is up to you to keep that in mind in difficult situations. You may even quell the fire completely by simply lending an ear and being supportive toward the learner. It is necessary at times, however, to refer these learners to behavioral experts in order to effectively help them deal with their issues. Having someone to support them along the way can speed up the recovery process and help the learners feel more safe.

Always Remain Calm and Courteous

It is important that you always remain calm and courteous in difficult situations, even in the face of danger or hostility. The problem with fighting fire with fire is that both parties will end up in flames. Instead of responding to anger with anger, neutralize the situation by keeping your composure and remaining calm. If you have to take a moment to compose yourself, then do so. Acknowledge that you need time to think and respond, rather than responding in the heat of the moment. This may take some time out of your lesson, but will ultimately be more beneficial in the long run. Take a breath if you need to, and remind yourself that you are the authority and are therefore responsible and in control.

Remember that you are the adult in the situation, and the learners ultimately look up to you. Rise above the situation and show the learners how they should respond in the face of confrontation and hostility. Never mock another learner, even if they are acting out. By mocking a learner, you are teaching the other learners that it is acceptable to mock their classmates. Humiliation is never a sustainable solution, and you may just lose that learner for the rest of their life. Furthermore, try not to appear condescending. This can be damaging to a learner's sense of worth and all the learners' level of respect for you. Learn to control your emotions. Doing so will help you to maintain these situations with poise and dignity, and you will be able to maintain the learners' respect in the process.

Instead of disrupting the entire class over a minor problem, try to minimize the minor problems or disruptions during the lesson. These are small and insignificant problems that don't cause too much disruption in the classroom. Use positive strategies when you deal with these situations, rather than yelling at learners or opting for punishment. A simple glance or direct question can go a long way to addressing minor problems without disrupting the class or drawing attention to the disruption. Proximity is also a very effective strategy for managing disruptive behavior. Standing close to a learner can be very intimidating, and they will likely stop their disruptive behavior immediately and shift their focus back to you. If the behavior persists, you may consider seating the learner close to your desk or close to another supportive learner that will help them rather than distracting them. If it is necessary to reprimand a learner, try to do so quickly and without too much disruption. Spending too much of your time and attention on a disruptive learner can worsen the situation and is often unnecessary, especially in the face of minor disruptions. Therefore, try to deal with problems as silently, quickly, and non-disruptively as possible. Wherever possible, try to speak to learners about their behavior privately. This not only prevents unnecessary disruptions in your lesson, but will save the learner plenty of humiliation in front of their classmates. Rather than addressing the learner in front of the whole class, pull them aside and speak to them privately. Humiliating the learner will simply cause them to drift away even further.

Most importantly, you need to encourage the rest of the learners to stay calm and embody a positive outlook on these situations and moments. Learners can easily be disrupted in moments like these, but by encouraging them to stay calm and positive, you are enabling them to control their responses to these situations. Make it a standard practice for everyone to come together and remind the disruptive learner how great of a friend, learner, or companion they are. This will likely calm the learner down and will strengthen the learner's sense of belonging and importance in the classroom. In light of such encouragement, it is difficult to stay angry or keep disrupting the classroom setting. Try at all times to set a positive tone in the classroom and model the appropriate response. One can easily react in a fit of anger, but taking the time to process and model the right response will not only contribute to your own personal growth, but will also contribute to the learners' personal growth, as they will likely learn from your reactions. Model the kind of behavior and reactions you expect from learners. We all know that learners tend to do what adults do, rather than what they say or ask. This is why it is important to model the expected behavior. You cannot simply voice your expectations and act however you wish, expecting the learners to follow your instructions. Your actions have to reflect your words.

Finally, help yourself to deal with misbehavior and processing negative feelings by reflecting back on past situations where a similar disruption or situation occurred. How did you deal with the situation then? What was the outcome? If the way in which you dealt with the situation did not help, try to identify why it didn't help and try to find a different way to deal with the situation. Reflective practice helps you to identify and learn from your mistakes and brainstorm future solutions.

Community Is Important!

It is of crucial importance to build a strong and supportive sense of community in the classroom. Be aware of your learners' cultural differences. Being aware of learners' cultural differences is more important than you may realize. In some cultures, for example, looking an elder in the eyes when they are addressed is considered disrespectful, whilst other cultures consider it a form of respect. You may think a learner is being disrespectful if they are looking down when you address them, but it might just be the exact opposite. These differences might seem small and insignificant, but they can have all the difference in the way you interpret learners' behavior. Be aware of these differences in your classroom, and respect learners' cultural differences. If necessary, read up on your learners' cultures in order to gain a better understanding of their practices and behaviors. You can even ask the learners to explain this to you themselves. Doing so will not only decrease the chances of unnecessary conflict erupting, but will also help your learners feel more accepted and respected, thus reducing the chances of them acting out in the first place. Create an environment that discourages the formation of cliques or any other antisocial behavior. This will help your learners feel more valued and important, and they will be less likely to misbehave or act out. By creating a sense of community, learners will also likely have more opportunity to talk about their troubles and whatever is bothering them. This will give them an output that does not result in disruption or misbehavior.

It is also important that you teach learners important social and personal skills that will improve their communication skills. These skills include both listening and speaking. Listening and speaking should be balanced out, as they are equally important in the communication process. It will also teach them to be more helpful and to share what they can with others when they can. Teach the learners important academic survival skills, such as paying attention, following directions, asking for help, and volunteering to answer. All these factors will help in their holistic development and will lessen the likelihood that they will act out. Teachers often take these skills for granted and assume that learners have picked these skills up somewhere in the learning process. Many learners have not, however, and end up struggling to learn, connect, and communicate as a result.

Ultimately, the way you treat your learners and the way you address them will determine whether they respect you. It may even have an impact on the frequency and severity of misbehavior and disruptions that occur in your classroom. Remember that a sense of belonging can go a long way to improving learners' development and behavior. Praise your learners regularly and sincerely to boost morale and encourage development and achievement. Focus on their improvements and their strengths. If a learner's behavior has improved or your class' behavior has improved notably, tell them.

Learners will likely behave themselves better in order to please you and gain your approval.

Chapter 5:

Online Teaching and 'The New Normal'

What a crazy time we live in. Considering all that has happened recently, being a teacher has definitely not become easier or any less complicated. With new and rapid technological developments and a sudden change in the way that teaching is conducted, the demands on teachers are becoming greater and greater. Teachers are expected to perform their regular teaching duties, provide support to learners, and keep up with the demands of the department, all while keeping up with the latest developments in technology and integrating these developments creatively into their lessons. This is definitely a lot to keep up with.

John Dewey said, "If we teach today's students as we taught yesterday's, we rob them of tomorrow." Considering recent and rapid advances in technology, and the integral role that it has taken in society, it is necessary and important that teachers integrate technology into their teaching approach regardless of the subject that they teach.

In contemporary society, teachers are not merely required to teach learners the syllabus anymore. Teachers are partially responsible for integrating learners into society, and this includes teaching them about the various features and capabilities that accompany technology. Along with that, however, learners should also be taught about the dangers and responsibilities that accompany the use of technology. There are no explicit school subjects that necessarily cover these important topics, and it is therefore up to teachers—all teachers—to teach the learners about these aspects of technology.

Other than that, it is important that teachers should focus on developing their more impersonal teaching skills. The concept sounds absurd, but recent developments have revealed the importance of being able to teach from a distance. Teaching has never been more complex! Online teaching is becoming increasingly popular, even necessary, in some places. The outbreak of new and terrifying pandemics, along with the complexities of modern society has made online teaching a more serious consideration and viable option. It is therefore important that you keep up with the latest improvements and developments in technology. Showcasing your creativity has never been more important, or necessary, than it is right now.

Being prepared for online development and presentation will definitely put you ahead of the game, heed my words.

Understanding Technology

First things first, you need to make sure that you understand technology and know all you need to know. This is a very important thing to consider. Be honest with yourself when considering this question. Being truthful will help you and will only benefit you moving forward. Ask yourself whether you need to take a course or engage with other, more "tech-savvy" teachers in order to be fully prepared for teaching. Are you so clued up and skilled that you would be able to teach someone else? You should be! If not, there are plenty of free courses online that can help.

I would like to take a moment to consider the five stages of learning that have been used in educational psychology and sports coaching, as I believe they have some significance. These stages have been discussed by Chris Drew (2020). You can use these five levels or stages to evaluate your technological competency levels and determine how much training or additional help is needed. The ultimate goal is to get to the fifth level of learning.

The first of these levels of learning is called unconscious incompetence and can be summarized as "I don't know that I don't know." At this stage, the subject is unconsciously incompetent. They know nothing about the subject, but they also don't know that they know nothing. They are oblivious and ignorant to the topic. Subjects may feel frustrated or confused with the topic, and struggle to see the significance or relevance of the topic. Many traditional, more experienced teachers have recently found themselves at this stage in terms of technology. Hopefully, you have moved past this stage, especially given the recent developments in education and world events.

The second stage is referred to as conscious incompetence, in other words, "I know that I don't know." At this stage the person becomes aware of their own ignorance and inabilities and develops a desire to learn more. A person may feel frustrated at their incompetence or unsure about how to go about learning about the particular topic. It can also incite motivation to learn about the topic, however, which will drive the desire to learn. You may be at this stage in your understanding of technology. With all that is going on, you may have realized that technology is important and necessary in education. If so, there are plenty of free courses, Youtube videos, and human resources at your disposal. Don't feel discouraged!

The third level of learning is conscious competence. This stage can be summarized as "I know how to do it, but I have to concentrate on my task." This involves being able to do a task independently and without support. Subjects can navigate the content or topic on their own, but still need to focus on the task in order to do it effectively and with minimal errors. It has not yet been established in their reflexive memory. Emotions may include hopefulness and determination after seeing results. It could also produce a sense of awkwardness, however, when subjects need to focus or pause to figure something out. Many teachers are at this level when it comes to understanding technology. They are able to use technology sufficiently, but sometimes get stuck or make mistakes. If you are at this stage, you are doing well. You may often refer to more experienced colleagues for assistance, or even watch a Youtube video explaining how to address a certain issue.

The fourth stage of learning is unconscious competence and can be described as "I can do it with ease and habitually." At this stage, subjects are able to carry out a task without too much effort or struggle. The task has become habitual, and they don't have to concentrate too hard to complete it. These people are comfortable completing the task and it may even become like second nature. These people are often experts in their field. If this is you, then I lift my hat to you. You are able to integrate technology effectively and creatively without the need to think too much or ask for help. Online teaching should be a breeze, but you are not yet at the top tier of learning.

The fifth and final level of learning is called conscious unconscious competence. This one sounds like a real tongue twister. The level can be summarized as "I can explain how I do it with ease to others." This level involves the ability to reflect on their tasks and abilities and to teach others how to complete the task. This is where the teachers come in. This requires subjects to be conscious of how they do a task whilst being able to complete the task with ease. If you are at this stage, then you are a true master and teacher.

Let Go of Perfectionism

My dad always says that technology is great when it works. When using technology, however, we very often suffer from technical glitches and connection problems, among other things. Just as you would flow through a normal classroom lesson, improvising and adapting where necessary, your online classroom will require the same approach. Online classrooms will have their own hiccups and interruptions, but as a teacher you need to be prepared for anything. Make sure that you know the work well enough that you can carry on fluently and without interruption, even if the PowerPoint you planned to use disappears or you accidentally delete your typed notes. Remember that you are allowed to learn alongside your learners. You do not need to be an expert, so long as you keep learning and growing. Online learning can be challenging for many, and stressing about having to conduct lessons perfectly will take away some of your much-needed energy from your lessons. If something goes wrong during your lessons, have the grace to forgive yourself and learn the appropriate solution for the next time you encounter the issue. Keep a brace face and fake it until you make it.

Remember that although you are conducting your lesson online, you still want to provide the learners with an authentic and engaging classroom environment. Where possible, try to involve your learners and have them participate in the lesson. Ask them to answer questions or comment on something you said. You can even ask them to provide an example or summarize your lesson. There are plenty of ways to get your learners involved and active.

Consider Learners' Equity of Access

Working online is easier for some than it is for others. This is a factor that is easily overlooked, especially when online learning is the only way to move forward. Keep in mind, however, that learners come from different financial, cultural, and socio-economic backgrounds. In the classroom, it is easy to lend a learner your textbook or give them an extra pencil. You can easily walk over to their desk and assist them if they need help. With online learning, these needs and shortcomings are not as easily identifiable. Remember that, despite it being the 21st century, not all learners have equal access to the necessary tools for online learning.

Not all the learners have access to internet connection or even a technological device they can use. Some learners have uncapped wireless connections, while other learners have to pay for the specific amount of data they need. Some learners cannot even afford basic amenities, let alone a technological device or the necessary amount of data needed for learning. Some areas may not have the necessary network coverage that learners need to connect, and these learners will inevitably lose out on much of the learning process. These are all things we so easily take for granted. Keep in mind that the majority of your learners will be accessing your content from a mobile phone. It is therefore important to ensure that your content and learning platforms are compatible with mobile devices.

Furthermore, not all learners have the same level of digital literacy. Some learners aren't as informed about the use of technology and technological devices as others. It may even be possible that some learners have never used a computer due to a lack of access or opportunity. For some learners, the only computer they will ever access is one that is used in their school. Some learners can type faster than others due to the difference in experience and access. Remember that some learners may never have needed to use a computer, or they rarely have a need for it. You can accommodate these learners by establishing flexible deadlines or an extended timeframe for the completion of typed responses or activities. If applicable, also keep special education learners in mind when you plan your online classroom. Learners with special educational needs still need to be accommodated and considered when you plan your learning and assessment activities.

These are necessary things to consider when planning your online curriculum and determining the way you will conduct your classes. There are a number of ways in which you can accommodate these learners and make provision for them. Flexible deadlines will help the learners to make the necessary plans to get their work done and submit their work on time.

Furthermore, planning interactive coursework will help the learners to engage with the work effectively and authentically. It might also be a good idea to provide the learners with access to additional support materials. These materials can range from study skills support to tutorial videos on how to access certain devices or websites. When you create online tasks, make sure you give learners enough time to complete these. Consider giving learners at least 24 hours to complete an online task or activity, even if it is a classroom activity. This will definitely go a long way to helping the learners cope better and be able to keep up with the learning process. You will also help to reduce the amount of stress and pressure they may be feeling as a result of online teaching and learning.

Set Clear Expectations

Set clear expectations with regards to the learning environment. This can include a range of expectations, including what learners can expect from you and what you expect from the learners. Communicate assessment due dates and deadlines as early as possible, so learners can plan in advance. Tell the learners and parents how frequently they can expect communication from you and inform them clearly of your office hours and availability. Tell the learners how much participation you will expect from them and which platforms they will be required to participate in. Finally, communicate with your learners as to what kind of conduct you expect from them in online classes and on your various learning platforms. Setting clear expectations and communicating these clearly reduces much of the anxiety that goes along with online learning—for you as well as for the learners and their parents. It removes much of the uncertainty and will help learners and parents feel more secure in the learners' educational needs.

Think Before You Write

Remember that any written text is open to interpretation and can be misunderstood very easily. It is therefore important that you carefully consider any written form of communication or written response before you send it. Try to maintain a clear, simple, and polite tone as far as possible. Make sure that you leave nothing open to interpretation. There are a number of things that you need to consider in order to communicate clearly and concisely.

The first step is to determine your audience. Are you writing to parents, learners, or peers? Consider what it is you need to communicate. Have the readers received prior communication about the topic, or is it a completely new topic? What is it that they need to know? How important is the topic to them? How interested might they be in what you have to say? While you are writing or responding, convey only the essential points. Stick to basic English in order to avoid any misunderstanding or misinterpretation. Don't use unnecessarily verbose statements or complex wording. You want the message to be as clear and concise as possible. Make sure that whatever jargon you decide to use, the readers will understand. If not, try to use simpler terms instead. Keep in mind that your learners and their parents might not understand certain education-related concepts or concepts related to your field of study. Therefore, keep your communications with learners and parents simple and easy to understand.

Make your main message a clear one. Keep your main discussion points in mind and make sure that the reader knows exactly what you are trying to say. Keep your sentences short and simple. A complex or unclear structure might make it more difficult for the reader to understand the message of your writing. Avoid cliches and unnecessary figurative languages. Pay attention to the structure of your writing. If possible, stick to the main questions of who, what, where, when, why, and how? This will help you to communicate your message clearly and concisely. Beware of drifting or deviating from the message you are trying to convey, as this will affect the reception of your communication.

Finally, proofread every piece of writing you send. If possible, ask someone you trust to read it and tell you what they understood. This will ensure that your message is clear and understandable. Make sure that you provide enough time to proofread without undue pressure, as this may lead you to miss some errors in your writing.

Video Content Goes a Long Way

Providing the learners with video content helps to maintain some sense of connection, even though the learners aren't able to be in the class. By recording video content, the learners can still sense your enthusiasm and energy. They will be able to see your face even though you aren't physically there with them. You'd be surprised at how your virtual presence and friendly face can comfort learners and ease their anxiety about the content. Recording videos will also help to keep the learning process more interactive and life-like. There's a reason kids would rather watch *Dora the Explorer* and *Mickey Mouse ClubHouse* than read a book about the same content. Videos give learners some sense of interaction and excitement. Videos can also be rewatched if need be, and learners can recap content or clarify misunderstandings easily.

You may even schedule a live session every now and again, depending on your learners' accessibility. There are plenty of free platforms such as Zoom and Microsoft Teams that allow you to host a video conference. These tools allow you to share audio and video, so you can see and hear your learners in real time. This is very useful if you want to host a live question and answer session or if you prefer to have a more engaging session. Learners are able to engage and interact in real time, and can even ask questions during the lesson if they need to. If learners are unable to access their microphone, you can use the chat option to ask and answer questions. The possibilities are endless. Using live sessions will help your classroom feel more like a physical classroom, and learners will feel more connected to the learning environment.

Use internet resources that are already available to provide extra support and additional information for your learners. If you come across a video or article that is interesting and relates to the content you are dealing with, send it to the learners. You may even refer them to websites that provide additional information and support on the content you are teaching. This will significantly lessen the load on you to create extra support material. Teach learners to be able to spot good content and false information so they can learn to use the internet responsibly and wisely. Sharing additional information and articles will also help to pique the learners' interest in the topic and will help to develop critical thinking skills among the learners. They will be able to engage more effectively with the content and will learn the value of reflective learning.

Create a Social Media Community

Social media is a great way to connect with your learners. It has become like a second language to 21st century youths. Their language is tainted with social media lingo and it forms a key part of many of their conversations. Use this to your advantage. Create a social media community in which you can connect with your learners and they can connect with one another.

There are countless tools that you can use to engage with learners. WhatsApp is a great and relatively cost-effective tool to help you keep in touch with learners. You can make announcements and send reminders about important events or activities. Learners can also use this platform to ask questions about content or activities, or to inform you of any challenges they may be having. This is also a great platform that you can use for quick clarifications if you identify any misconceptions. Learners can respond to questions or post their own contributions using GIFs, images, or voice notes. Emojis allow them to express themselves more creatively. Platforms like TikTok can be used to make educational content in a way that is fun and engaging. You can ask the learners to create and share TikTok videos where they explain certain aspects of the content or showcase certain skills. The possibilities are truly endless.

You may even wish to create a separate platform to engage with parents. Sending emails can be long, tedious, and frankly, unreliable on occasion. Some parents rarely read their emails, whilst others claim to have never received them. Some parents may not even have an existing email address. Getting hold of parents via email can therefore be a difficult and tedious process. By adding your learners' parents into one WhatsApp group, you can be sure that they are, in fact, receiving your messages. Use WhatsApp groups to communicate important information or send reminders.

You may even communicate with certain parents individually if you are concerned about a learner. Whatsapp provides you with easy access to the parents, and if they do not respond to your messages, you can always phone them. This platform provides an opportunity for parents to ask questions if they have any concerns or need clarification on anything. It is a sustainable and effective way to keep in touch with parents regarding what is happening at the school and in the virtual classroom without having to answer countless emails and phone calls.

When you are communicating, use various platforms to share information. Provide your email address and your phone number to ensure that learners and teachers are able to reach you in any way they can afford to or have the means to. Make sure to communicate your office hours clearly to avoid those middle-of-the-night phone calls and to ensure that your weekends remain yours. Make sure that you stick to these hours and are consistent in keeping them. Answer messages only during your office hours, and if parents phone you outside office hours ask them to phone you back during the specified time. This is an important part of maintaining your independence and keeping your work life separate from your personal life. If you don't separate your personal life from your work life, you will inevitably suffer from burnout.

Keep the Creativity Flowing

Being creative is an important part of your classroom practice. Don't allow the limitations of having to teach online limit your creativity and shift you into automatic gear. There are countless opportunities for creativity, even with online learning. The more creative your lessons are, the more likely learners are to engage, enjoy and remember what you have taught. Janet Taylor (2020) suggests three different categories of creative thinking that you need to consider in your lessons. These are directed toward art teaching, but can be applied in any subject area with some adaptation.

1. *Creative Boosts*

Creative boosts are activities that are quick, fun, and engaging. These can be used to engage your learners in thought and can promote experimentation among learners. They are usually one-day or once-off activities that will give learners' creativity a boost. These exercises or activities can be centered around inquiry-learning to encourage the learners to take control of their own learning experiences and explore the content more autonomously. You may even use activities such as a scavenger hunt, where learners are encouraged to seek the answers for themselves and piece the content together to create a bigger picture.

There are some things to keep in mind when using creative boosts in your lessons. Firstly, keep your final outcomes in mind. If you haven't yet taught the learners about this particular unit or topic, you cannot expect them to piece the clues together 100% accurately. Be gracious and understanding in these cases. Secondly, set up some new expectations. In creative boosts, it is important to communicate your expectations clearly so the learners can know exactly what you are expecting from them for the activity. Finally, remember that if learners are required to explore materials and resources at home, this might take longer than you expect. It is easier for learners to engage with materials in the classroom, since they have you to guide them. Exploring materials on their own can be much more difficult, and learners will therefore need more time to do this. Provide learners with a reasonable timeline to complete research activities.

2. Creative Constraints

Creative constraints may be a bit more abstract and difficult to plan. These are intended to challenge the learners' capabilities and push their boundaries. You may, for example, ask learners to suggest possible ways in which a historical problem could have been avoided or better dealt with, construct something completely new, or find new uses for materials or objects. These activities take longer to do and are intended to promote creative and critical thinking in new and innovative ways.

There are innumerable opportunities when incorporating creative constraints in your lessons. Firstly, you may prompt your learners to consider real situations without putting constraints on themselves or their capabilities. Even though these exercises may be based on hypothetical or fictional scenarios, there are real considerations for the learners to keep in mind. Remind the learners that there are still real-life factors to consider. Secondly, you might try giving the learners a fantastical problem, asking them to identify possible choices along with the existing constraints. Finally, you may consider giving learners a limited choice of materials to create something new. Rather than specifying the materials they are required to use, specify how much of one specific material they may use. This enables them to use whatever they have at their disposal, and do so creatively. Doing so will therefore foster innovative thinking and creative problem solving abilities in the learner.

3. *Creative Sparks*

Creative sparks provide learners with a push of creativity that inspire learners to work on a particular piece of writing, art, or construction. Creative sparks involve short exercises, ranging from fifteen minutes to a full day, aimed at inspiring movement, creative thinking, collection of information, and engagement with their piece. Although this is focused on creative construction and art, it can be adapted and applied to any subject. It may involve a piece of writing in some subjects and the creation of a creative model or illustration in other subjects.

There are some tips that you may wish to consider when incorporating creative sparks into your lesson. Give your learners a series of sparks to choose from. Based on your choices, learners can then decide on whichever spark inspires or interests them the most, and use that as their project topic. This provides the learners with some flexibility in terms of choice and allows the learners to explore what interests them. It will also make your job significantly less boring, since not all learners will be presenting or submitting on the exact same topic. Creative sparks are an effective way to demonstrate the creative process. Whilst planning their project, learners use sparks as the basis for their ideas and documentation. Theory will rely on these sparks throughout the process of creating, writing, or constructing. Finally, give your learners a choice of media. Allow learners a choice in how they present their final product or findings. These may include videos, audio, posters, or even a timelapse. This allows the learners to engage in further creative thinking and will make the project significantly more interesting for both you and the learner. Learners are able to explore the content on their own terms, and will likely engage with the content more effectively. Doing so also considers learners' different learning styles and creates a platform where all learners can excel.

These are just some of the ways in which you can incorporate creativity in your lessons. These creative categories are a great way to encourage discovery learning and innovative thinking. By using these strategies, or other similar strategies, you will be enabling learners to become autonomous learners and to widen their horizons significantly. You will also be illustrating to the learners that the content can be understood and applied in a wide variety of ways. Learners will be encouraged to engage with the content in a way that interests them.

Another suggestion of using online learning creatively is creating a Bitmoji classroom. This is a new trend among teachers and is a brilliant way to engage your learners creatively. This involves designing a Bitmoji, a cartoon replica, of themselves. Teachers then create a virtual classroom by using Google Slides. They use this platform to create an image of the inside of a classroom, featuring a desk, whiteboard, and even some posters. There are numerous props that you can add to your classroom. Once finished, you then add your

Bitmoji into the class using the Bitmoji Extension on your browser and voila! You have created a virtual, cartoon version of your classroom. From here, you can add books onto your virtual bookshelf with links to readings and assignments. You can add details to the whiteboard and even upload pictures of learners' work to hang on your virtual wall. This is a great way to make learners' feel more at home in their online environment and a fun way for you to engage with learners.

There are countless online tools that will help you to keep the online environment fun, exciting, and engaging. These are but a few examples. By using creativity in your online learning environment, you are likely to spark the learners' interests, make them feel more at ease, and make the learning experience a lot more fun. You will also be teaching the learners something about technology in the process.

Let the Learners Do the Work

Tracking learners' progress can be difficult in an online setting. Checking whether learners are, in fact, doing their work can be time-consuming and tedious. It can be tempting to want to take the wheel, especially if you are a control freak. Doing so will be to the learners' detriment, however. Micromanaging the online environment can be very limiting to the learners' learning experience, and you may become the very thing that is preventing the learners from having an optimal learning experience. Remember that the aim of learning is maximum participation and engagement over the maximum period of time. It is therefore essential that you involve the learners and allow them to do the work.

Ask the learners and parents for feedback on the learning experiences. This will help you to continually improve and optimize your teaching practice and, consequently, their learning experience. Feedback can be extremely valuable and insightful, and it is always a good idea to heed any advice you might receive. Feedback can cover anything from content to teaching methods, as well as areas that need improvement. You can use various platforms for feedback, such as an online discussion board or even an anonymous online form. Anonymity might spur learners on to provide true and critical feedback, rather than merely complimenting your styles for fear of being identified. Involving learners in feedback will ensure that they feel valued and appreciated—true stakeholders of the learning process.

Have a closing activity for each lesson that you conduct. This ensures that learners remain focused and attentive during the lesson. Using an "exit ticket" is a great way to ensure that learners have attended the session and are paying attention to what you are saying. The exit ticket strategy involves learners doing and submitting an activity as their exit ticket from the class. If learners have not done the activity, they cannot exit the class. These activities can also be used to track learners' progress and understanding of the content. It involves the learners in the lesson, rather than making the lesson a teacher-centered event. Ending the lesson with a closing activity helps the learners to reflect on what they have learned and burns it into the back of their heads. They are then more likely to remember the gist of the lesson. Briefly recap your learning objectives at the end of the lesson to ensure that learners know what they should be taking away from the lesson. If learners are unsure of one of the outcomes, you can reiterate it or ask another learner to explain.

Have your learners engage with the content outside of the lesson time by extending the discussion to other platforms. Have learners discuss the content with one another. You may even have learners explain the content to one another. Ask learners to create examples or host critical discussions about the implications of the content you have taught. This will not only help the learners engage more effectively, but they will also develop critical inquiry skills that will help them later on in life.

You may even consider asking certain learners to share something during the online lesson. This can make your job much easier and gives the learners a sense of importance in the classroom. Have your learners create a skit using videos that you can share in class time or ask some of the learners to read excerpts of important texts. Keep in mind that learners have different learning styles. This does not change in an online classroom. It is therefore important that you use various online platforms that cater for a variety of learning styles and stimulate learners' different senses. Make use of both group and individual projects and assessments. This might lessen the workload that learners have to deal with as well as teach them the importance of group work. Giving the learners group assessments will also ensure that learners' stay connected with their peers and maintain a sense of community.

A Great Teacher Is a Great Teacher

Teaching online may be a new and challenging experience for you, but remember that what makes you a great teacher will transfer to your online environment. You are just as important and brilliant in the virtual classroom environment as you are in the physical classroom environment. Being a great teacher comes from more than just knowing what to do in the classroom. Your passion, enthusiasm, and dedication to the profession is what makes you a great teacher, and these things don't simply change when your environment changes. Whenever you feel overwhelmed, remember to set clear goals and communicate your expectations to the learners. These are the two most important things to remember. The rest will come naturally and with time.

Make time for yourself where you can reflect on how the teaching and learning process is going. Perfection is not expected, but improvement is mandatory. Reflect on your experiences and identify areas that need improvement. You may consider asking yourself questions like:

- What activities do learners engage in more frequently and what are the possible reasons?
- What have I learned about my learners as a result of their participation in lessons?
- What improvements can I make to make the learning experience more inclusive, meaningful, and accessible to learners?
- How are my learners doing mentally, physically, and emotionally?
- How am I doing mentally, physically, and emotionally?

Taking the time to reflect helps you to slow down and have a realistic look at your classroom. Only by taking the time to reflect will you be able to identify the obstacles in your learning process.

Very importantly, foster relationships with each of your learners. Learners may feel lost in a big group, especially in an online learning environment. Making an effort to connect with your learners is important to ensure that they feel a sense of belonging or importance. You can accomplish this by providing individualized feedback to learners' activities or discussion contributions.

Chapter 6:

Managing Your Time Like a Boss

Time management is of cardinal importance when it comes to teaching. There is true power in being able to manage your time wisely and effectively, and it will help you to ensure that things go according to plan as far as possible. Being a teacher requires plenty of work and discipline. In planning your lesson, setting up assessments, and ensuring your learners keep up with the content, there is a lot that is expected of any teacher. With all the work that goes along with being a teacher, you may feel like there is not nearly enough time to get to everything done. The bad news—it is all up to you to make sure everything runs smoothly. The good news—it is all up to you to make sure everything runs smoothly. Your perspective is everything. This may seem like a lot of responsibility, but there are a number of positive things to also keep in mind.

In a sense, you are your own boss. There are certain regulations to adhere to, and there are always schedules and demands to keep up with, but how you manage your time is ultimately up to you. You can therefore use your time as you please. Keep in mind, however, that this also means that it is your responsibility to stay on top of everything. How you manage your time can have a tremendous impact on the way that you manage your life and how much time you have for that which is important to you. Learning effective time management skills will help you tremendously in managing your workload, being more productive, and providing your learners with the best education you can give them.

Be Strategic With Your Planning

Michael Altshuler said the following: "The bad news is time flies. The good news is you're the pilot." It's not how much time you have, but what you do with the time that you have that matters. There are a few important factors to consider when planning for your assignments, tests, and so on. It is not only the learners you need to take into consideration, but you also need to consider the load it will place on you. Don't overwhelm yourself unexpectedly with too much grading at once. This will exhaust you and place you under tremendous stress. Make sure you pace assessments in such a way that you will be able to mark them without undue stress or pressure. This will not only help you in terms of reducing the pressure you are under, but it will also ensure that you can mark fairly and considerately.

Look at the whole term, semester, or year and try to reverse engineer the assessments that require grading. Organize and schedule exams and important assessments first, then you can fill the time in-between with tests and quizzes. See where you have room for more grading and put the bigger assignments in those spaces. Take note, however, of your teaching schedule as well when you are scheduling these assessments. Remember that you cannot assess something you have not yet taught. It is therefore important that you consider your teaching schedule along with the time you require to grade assessments.

Be cognizant of the way you plan homework and class activities. Certain activities may need extra support and should therefore be conducted in class. Other activities, however, may simply be a repetition of what was learned during the lesson. These activities can be given as homework. Make sure you are using your designated lesson time optimally and providing the learners with effective and stimulating activities that will help to promote higher order reasoning skills. Make sure that by giving the learners homework, you aren't giving yourself more work. Have the learners mark one another's work or simply check for a parent's signature. Remember that not everything needs to be graded, and not everything needs to be graded by you. Having learners mark their own work or mark each other's work promotes reflective learning, and learners will be able to identify errors and mistakes more easily. You may even consider weekly homework an option.

Whatever you do, make sure that you are using your time wisely.

Prioritize your assessments and lessons according to the day, week, month, etc. Make sure that you provide room for the most important things first, and get those done, then you can schedule the other things. If you find that you don't get to the minor things, you can always try to make up for those later. Not only that, but you can organize your day based on your priorities. Prioritizing effectively will help you to deal more effectively with your tasks, focusing on the most important and urgent tasks first to ensure that you are meeting deadlines.

Start and End With a Purpose

Start the day by planning what you need to get done and identifying your priorities for the day. Spend a few moments to compose yourself and prepare yourself for the day. Run through everything you have to get done that day, and take a moment to plan your day. This will not only start off your day on a positive note, but it helps you prepare for your day. Starting your day with a purpose prevents unnecessary distractions and helps you to cope better with unexpected events or occurrences.

You may consider "theming" your days. Designate specific days of the week to specific major tasks, and then you can add or integrate other minor tasks into your week as well. You may spend Mondays doing lesson planning, for example, and Tuesdays checking workbooks. This is a great way to ensure that routine tasks don't get neglected.

Be Aware of Challenges Before They Arise

There are a few challenges and obstacles that you need to be aware of when it comes to time management. Some tasks that teachers need to complete can take up a lot of time and energy, and it is important that you be aware of these threats and how to combat them.

1. Designing Lessons and Assessments

Designing assessment tasks, lessons, and lesson plans is an essential part of teaching. These tasks can be time consuming and even tedious at times, but they cannot be avoided. If designing lessons and assessments is taking up too much of your time, you may try turning to other sources. There are countless resources on the internet that will provide you with inspiration, tips, and even content for lesson planning. Some websites offer free resources to teachers, while others require membership payment. Whatever route you decide to take, there are countless places on the internet that will provide you with the inspiration and the tools you need to complete these tasks more effectively.

You may even consider using other teachers as a resource, too. Ask your colleagues about their experiences and ideas they have used in their lesson and assessment planning. It might spark some inspiration for your next lesson. You can still create your own assessments and design your own lessons, but turning to other sources will save you much time when it comes to brainstorming and the design process.

2. Socializing at Work

Picture this—you have a double free period coming up, the perfect and much needed opportunity to catch up on work. You have it all planned out. You want to finish setting up the exam you have been putting off for so long and send it for moderation. Then, you want to create some much needed remediation worksheets for the learners to serve as revision for their upcoming exam. You still have a few books to check before the end of the day, and you promised Lisa you would look at her essay draft. The bell rings and you walk to the staff room. You are going to make yourself a nice, big cup of coffee and get to work. There's no time to waste. In the staff room, you run into one of your colleagues whom you haven't seen in a long while. You start chatting while you make your coffee and, before you know it, the bell rings! You've missed a whole period of admin time.

I'm sure you have experienced this. Socializing is just too hard not to do. While socializing and spending time with friends and colleagues is important, there are also a number of things that need to get done. Time is precious, and you should use it wisely. If you know that you have a lot of work to get done, make sure you stay away from the temptation to socialize. Find a quiet space where you can work without interruptions and without the need to make small talk. Avoid the staffroom and close the door to your office. That way, you can make certain that you get your work done with minimal distractions.

3. Nonessential Materials

As teachers, we tend to get caught up in teaching material and extra resources. We try to focus on all the content at once and end up with a ton of materials and paperwork. We find so many resources online or elsewhere that can be useful and informative, and eventually end up with a boatload of materials. When you plan your lessons, make sure you are focusing on the outcomes that you are planning to achieve.

Anything more than that is extra. Evaluate your lessons, and get rid of any unnecessary or excessive material that doesn't focus on your lesson's outcomes. This will ensure that your lessons are impactful and educational, and will get rid of any unnecessary paperwork you may have.

4. Parent and Learner Meetings

Meetings with parents can be long and drawn out. Some meetings are downright unnecessary. It is therefore important that you prepare thoroughly for such meetings to guarantee that you waste no time on unnecessary explanations or searching for the necessary proof. Being prepared helps you stay within the specified time frame and ensures that you don't get into unnecessary arguments with the parent.

Make sure that you have the learner's file, portfolio, and their grades on-hand during the meeting. Make a list of the things that you need to speak to the parent or learner about. Meeting with a parent can be scary, especially when the meeting was scheduled by the parent. By being prepared, however, you will be better equipped to conduct the meeting in a professional and timely manner, without unnecessary squabbles or quarrels.

5. *After-School Help*

Setting office hours to help learners is part of teaching. During your office hours, make sure that you are using the time to help the learner in such a way that they are able to continue the work on their own. Don't coddle them or give them exactly what you are looking for in an assignment. Rather, equip them to be able to navigate the assignment on their own. If you coddle the learner, they will likely return with more questions or for the next assignment. Make sure that you are equipping them to answer the same kind of question in the future, rather than simply helping them to answer this particular question.

You may have a large number of learners come to you during office hours. Try having the learners answer one another's questions while they are waiting for you. This may help solve some learners' questions and will significantly reduce the number of learners that end up needing your help. Another tactic you might try is to have learners with similar questions come in together. In this way you can address the problem once, and you won't have to waste time explaining the same thing over and over again.

6. Plan for Potential Crises

It is much better to plan ahead for any problems or crises that may arise than having them pop up unexpectedly and throwing you off guard. Urgent crises can easily distract teachers from that which is important. Planning ahead and scheduling your time wisely allows you to plan for potential crises as well. Be aware of any problems that may arise during a lesson, during a term or during the school year. Be aware of any problems that may hinder the teaching and learning process or that will slow down your work. Being aware of these problems will help you to be more prepared if they arise. Brainstorming potential solutions can help you think faster on your feet and take these distractions in stride.

It may also be a good idea to plan some extra time in your class schedule in case something comes up. Have some activities or strategies that you can implement if something comes up during class time. This will help you not to waste too much of your lesson time, and will ensure that the learners are not distracted.

Procrastination Is Poison

Catherine Pulsifier made a terrific point when she said the following: "Procrastinating does nothing more than add to your do list. Do it, be done with it!"

It can be so easy to procrastinate your work, especially if you've had a long and tiring day. Coming home and having to do more work seems daunting and even downright depressing. Some tasks may seem small and irrelevant, and leaving them for later often seems harmless. Procrastination may be a temporary solution, but things will start piling up quickly, and soon you will have more work than you can deal with. Soon a little tiredness will turn into full-blown panic and all-nighters.

Have a plan and stick to your plan. When you have received a pile of papers to grade, set a daily goal and divide your papers or assignments into smaller piles. Focusing on these smaller piles is significantly less daunting than having a stack of 150 assignments to work through. Planning is the most effective way to get things done on time and without too much pressure. Where possible, you can even try to get ahead of your plan. This will help you to make space for those days where you cannot keep up with your work. It may even provide some space for you to take a breather on the days when you feel tired or overwhelmed. It will also allow you to plan for many potential and unforeseen setbacks that may occur.

When you have small windows of time, take advantage of it. Use unexpected free time to tackle small tasks and projects or even get started on bigger ones. Getting these things ticked off of your schedule bit by bit can take a load off your back. You may even find yourself with some extra free time to spend with family or friends, or on something you love.

There are a number of ways in which you can avoid procrastination and remain focused. Being organized is one of the major things that will help. Using a planner or diary helps you to keep track of tasks you need to do and therefore keeps you on track and up-to-date. Setting simple daily goals can also help you to achieve more on a daily basis, without feeling the need to be busy constantly. Create a schedule to make sure that you remember important dates and deadlines coming up. This will help you not to procrastinate on those big, important tasks. For those tasks that don't have a deadline, set your own deadline. This will help to turn the indefinite inevitability of the task into something real and tangible. Get rid of any unnecessary distractions that might disrupt your work flow. This is one of the major causes of procrastination. Work in intervals to increase your productivity and successfully get your work done in an effective, timely manner without distractions. You will also ensure that you have enough rest time in between working spurts to prevent overworking yourself. Make time to take a break. Not taking a break can decrease your productivity and will increase the likelihood of procrastination. Incentives are always a great way to get something done. Use incentives to increase your productivity and get those undesirable tasks done. Focus on completing the hardest tasks first. It's easy to focus on other, smaller tasks when we don't feel like doing a certain task. The sad reality is, that task will inevitably have to be done, and it is better done sooner rather than later. Finally, tell someone about your goal. This introduces accountability and motivates you to achieve these goals.

Plan Realistically

Make sure that you are being realistic with yourself and with your plan. If you attempt to bite off more than you can chew you will inevitably become overwhelmed and will likely fall behind. When you plan, be realistic with yourself about what you can and cannot achieve in one day. Remember that your learners suffer as much from a loaded schedule as you do. Make sure you take your learners' workload and yours into consideration. Try to keep a to-do list for your week as well as having one for every day. That way, if something comes up, you can add it to your weekly list. During the day, however, you can focus on your daily tasks. This can prove more effective and far less intimidating. You may even consider keeping a teacher planner. This will help you keep all your bearings together and will allow you to keep most of your things in one place.

Ideally, keep between three to five items on your to-do list. This will help you to stay positive about being able to get these things done and make your tasks seem much more manageable. Three to five items is a manageable list that can be done, even on your busiest days. Make sure you write these items down and keep track of which ones you have completed. There is some satisfaction in being able to tick off things from your to-do list. Doing so reminds you of those things you have accomplished and that you have gotten things done today, no matter how busy or unproductive you may have felt.

As unorthodox and possibly selfish as this may sound, schedule your personal downtime as well. You may think this is unnecessary and that you'll make time to relax and breathe in between tasks or deadlines, but such a mindset will only lead to burnout and much suffering. Scheduling your downtime is not selfish or lazy, it simply means that you are deliberate about your well-being, and making time for yourself is a priority in your life. As a teacher with much to do, you can easily be tempted to use your free time for grading, feedback, or planning, but remember that there are other important priorities in your life as well. It is necessary and important to schedule time for your personal needs. This is important for your emotional, physical, and mental well-being. Exhausted teachers are less valuable in the classroom and are unable to function as they normally would. A teacher should be healthy, energetic, and refreshed, and the only way to do this is to take care of yourself, too.

Hide When You Can

This may sound bad, but you also need a breather. Close your office at certain times and ensure that you have some quiet time for your own productivity. If you are always spending time helping other people at your own expense, your work will inevitably suffer. Make sure that you are making time to spend on your own work and your priorities. When you have some free time or you are planning on getting some work done, close your office door to avoid chatty colleagues and unnecessary interruptions. You may even try putting a sign on your door that reads "Do not disturb" or "Work in progress." If someone does bother you even with this sign up, it will be about something urgent or important.

Create a Supportive Community

Use parent volunteers as frequently and as best as you can. They wouldn't be volunteering if they didn't want to help you, so go ahead and have them help. This will not only involve the community more, but it will take a huge load off of you. Delegating certain tasks to volunteers will enable you to focus on what is important and to get the most urgent tasks done without unnecessary distractions.

Creating a community is not only about utilizing volunteers. Build a network with other teachers around you, both to learn from them and to collaborate with them. Leaning on your colleagues can go a long way to helping you and creating a supportive community where you can thrive. If necessary, ask for help from other teachers. Delegate some of your tasks if they are willing, or collaborate with them to get mutual tasks done. If you find yourself in a pickle, you can turn to other teachers for advice, tips, and assistance on how to deal with certain things. They may even make certain tasks easier if they have done them before.

You may even want to build an accountability community. Team up with some of your colleagues or even a group of friends and set some rules on how to manage your time more effectively. Keep one another accountable and support one another regularly. You can even share some time management tips in the group that you found effective. This is a good way to build a support system that can empathize, but will also keep you accountable. It is a good platform for sharing experiences and therefore minimizing the trial and error period.

You can even consider using your learners' help—not in the major tasks, but in the everyday classroom tasks. This can make your job much easier and gives the learners a sense of importance in the classroom.

Learn to Say No!

I cannot highlight the value of this principle enough. It is tremendously important that you know when to say no. If you are a people pleaser, this may be even harder for you than it is for others. Saying no might often feel rude, unhelpful, or unprofessional. You may feel guilty over having to say no and find yourself saying yes instead. The problem with not being able to say no, however, is that your work tends to suffer. There is no use in being helpful and friendly all the time when you cannot even find the time to finish your own work. The catch is that when you are the one always agreeing to help others, people will continue coming to you for help. Soon you won't be able to keep up with all the work and you will eventually burn out.

Steve Jobs said the following: "It's only by saying NO that you can concentrate on the things that are really important." You need to make time for the things that are important, and if saying yes to others doesn't do that, you need to say no. If something does not fit into your schedule or your flow, it's okay to say no. Don't throw away your own precious time because of someone else. Your priorities and your time is the most important. You get to choose how you use your time and what you want to spend it on. Make sure that whatever you are saying yes to is worth your time and effort, and that you can afford to take it on.

Conclusion

This book has taught you everything you need to know about being the best teacher you can be. It has hopefully quelled any fears or anxieties you may have had by equipping you with essential tools to be a strong, enthusiastic, and successful teacher.

In this book, I have highlighted the importance of the first day. I have provided you with a list of preparation tips that you need to have a successful and exciting first day. I have also shown you what you need to do to keep your learners' attention. By applying the various strategies and techniques I have discussed in this book, you will be able to effectively maintain the learners' attention throughout your lesson. Keep in mind that all learners are different, and not all techniques are effective for each type of learner. Getting to know your learners and their needs will help you to identify the most appropriate strategy for your classroom. By making your learners feel involved, valued, and important, you will be able to create a more conducive learning environment for all your learners. I have therefore provided you with a number of factors and strategies to consider that will help you make your learners feel valued and important in your classroom. Ultimately, this will improve learners' academic performance and lead to personal and social growth in their lives.

Part of being a teacher is being able to navigate unexpected and unimaginable events or crises in the classroom. Reacting in outrage or condescension will only lead to the learners disrespecting or even fearing you. I have therefore provided you with a whole chapter of tips, tricks, and strategies that will help you navigate the unimaginable. By considering these steps and strategies, you will be more equipped to deal with these instances as they occur. In today's day and age, being able to navigate an online classroom has become part and parcel of the teaching profession. This book has provided you with all you need to know about being able to navigate your online learning environment. I have shown you how to create the optimal learning environment that will foster autonomous learning and ensure that learners are able to keep up with the syllabus. Finally, this book has discussed all the important aspects of time management. This is an essential part of creating a structured professional life, especially given the demands of the teaching profession. By applying what you have learned in the final chapter of this book, you will be able to manage your time like a boss.

Remember that a teacher is never really fully equipped or completely clued up. Teaching is about growth, and there is always more to learn. Even the most experienced teacher has not learned all there is to know about teaching. So gear up! You're in for a bumpy, but very rewarding ride. It may be true that teachers work many, many more hours than they are required to. It is definitely not a half-day job, as some believe it to be. I promise you, however, that it is one of the most rewarding and satisfying professions out there. One day you will be able to sit back and truly say that you've made a difference, and that is worth all the trouble in the world.

Thank you for taking the time to read this book. I hope it has been as edifying reading this book as it has been writing it. I have learned so much in the process of writing this book, and I truly hope it has changed your perspective on teaching. Please do not hesitate to leave a favorable review so other teachers like you can find this valuable, life-changing resource.

I would like to leave you with the following inspirational words by Henry Brooks Adams: "Teachers affect eternity; no one can tell where their influence stops."

References

108 procrastination quotes. (n.d.). Inspirational Words of Wisdom. https://www.wow4u.com/procrastination/#:~:text=%20108%20Procrastination%20Quotes%20%201%20Procrastinating%20does

3M. (2000). *Polishing your presentation*. http://web.archive.org/web/20001102203936/http://3m.com/meetingnetwork/files/meeting_guide_pres.pdf

Anderson, M. (2016, August 29). *45 Routines to teach in the first weeks of school*. Mike Anderson Consulting. https://leadinggreatlearning.com/45-routines-teach-first-weeks-school/?doing_wp_cron=1595775987.6335699558258056640625

Ankucic, M. (2020, January 2). *10 Simple ways to nail the first day of the new school year*. 3P Learning. https://www.3plearning.com/blog/10-simple-ways-nail-first-day-new-school-year/

Assertiveness - An introduction. (2011). SkillsYouNeed. https://www.skillsyouneed.com/ps/assertiveness.html

Barile, N. (2016, December 8). *Mastering the parent-teacher meeting: Eight powerful tips.* Hey Teach! https://www.wgu.edu/heyteach/article/mastering-parent-teacher-meeting-eight-powerful-tips1612.html

Barile, N. (2020, March 9). *5 Major time management challenges for teachers and how to avoid these time sucks.* Hey Teach! https://www.wgu.edu/heyteach/article/5-major-time-management-challenges-teachers-and-how-avoid-these-time-sucks1803.html

Blad, E. (2017, June 20). *Students' sense of belonging at school is important. It starts with teachers.* Education Week. https://www.edweek.org/ew/articles/2017/06/21/belonging-at-school-starts-with-teachers.html

Carter, A. (2015, October 27). *The importance of classroom rules.* Education.Co.Za. https://education.co.za/the-importance-of-classroom-rules

Collins, R. (2019). *Top 10 ways to avoid procrastination.* College Express. https://www.collegexpress.com/articles-and-advice/majors-and-academics/blog/top-10-ways-avoid-procrastination/

Cooper, S. (2016, September 24). *10 Best practices to be an effective online teacher.* eLearning Industry.

https://elearningindustry.com/10-best-practices-effective-online-teacher

Crockett, R. (2016, July 30). *Giving student feedback: 7 Best practices for success*. Global Digital Citizen Foundation. https://globaldigitalcitizen.org/giving-student-feedback-7-best-practices?__hstc=71880012.6427937570a6caea1bd5416ae85c45fe.1557270570516.1579505608848.1579512153627.239&__hssc=71880012.7.1579512153627&__hsfp=1835653276

Drew, C. (2020). *5 Stages of learning (Levels of learning ladder)*. Helpful Professor. https://helpfulprofessor.com/stages-of-learning/#:~:text=By%20Chris%20Drew%2C%20PhD.%20In%20educational%20psychology%20and

Emphasis. (2009, January 29). *Simple strategies for clear written communication, the actuary*. https://www.writing-skills.com/simple-strategies-for-clear-written-communication-the-actuary

Esquer, J. (2020, March 23). *The power of breath*. Oxygen Magazine. https://www.oxygenmag.com/the-oxygen-challenge/the-power-of-breath

Goodreads. (n.d.). *Time management quotes (610 quotes)*. https://www.goodreads.com/quotes/tag/time-management

Graber, D. (2014, February 28). *Kids, tech and those shrinking attention spans*. Huffpost. https://www.huffpost.com/entry/kids-tech-and-those-shrinking-attention-spans_b_4870655?guccounter=1&guce_referrer=aHR0cHM6Ly9zZWFyY2gueWFob28uY29tL w&guce_referrer_sig=AQAAANCueQhXPtMIw-ApqhrI9M6RIeeSSNGcAVxLTahWDU5_ljQ2z47ecWUL752FoguUUc8ocozGIzOkR7g4RRWWVGEcZoJA6KhoHeRh8vibIXA9uIZbXaWGz22k42PXblTpzbu8KcBLZ5y5o44l6Df4MBihNmxUpsX4u_Lxceie-lVt

Guest Blogger. (2014, December 16). *How to make your students feel valued as individuals*. The Inspired Classroom. https://theinspiredclassroom.com/2014/06/make-students-feel-valued-individuals/

Ho, L. (2018, March 6). *Your night routine guide to sleeping better & waking up productive*. Lifehack. https://www.lifehack.org/679044/night-routine-ultimate-guide

Horton, J. (2019, January 3). *10 Time management secrets from teachers who are living their best lives*. WeAreTeachers. https://www.weareteachers.com/teacher-time-management-secrets/

Kallio, C. (2020, March 7). *Why having a morning routine is important*. WorkingMyMind.

https://workingmymind.com/why-having-a-morning-routine-is-important/#:~:text=Why%20having%20a%20morning%20routine%20is%20important.%20Simply

Kriegel, O. (2020, August 17). *How to nail the first week of school: Tips for a new teacher.* Hey Teach! https://www.wgu.edu/heyteach/article/how-to-nail-the-first-week-of-school-tips-for-a-new-teacher1808.html

Lee, C. (2019, April 16). *7 ways to give your students a sense of belonging.* Turnitin.Com. https://www.turnitin.com/blog/7-ways-to-give-your-students-a-sense-of-belonging

Linsin, M. (n.d.). *The 7 rules of handling difficult students.* Smart Classroom Management. https://www.smartclassroommanagement.com/2011/04/23/7-rules-of-handling-difficult-students/

Lynette, R., & Noack, C. (2012, April 17). *20 ways to keep your students' attention.* Minds in Bloom. https://minds-in-bloom.com/20-ways-to-keep-your-students-attention/

Managing difficult teaching situations – Office of teaching & learning. (n.d.). University of Denver. https://otl.du.edu/plan-a-course/teaching-resources/managing-difficult-teaching-situations/

Martinez, D. N., & Contributor, L. (2019, May 5). *Learning to say "no" quotes even when it's not easy.* Everyday Power. https://everydaypower.com/say-no-quotes/#:~:text=Learning%20to%20say%20%E2%80%9CNo%E2%80%9D%20Quotes%20Even%20When%20It%E2%80%99s

Nannini, C. (2018, July 27). *How to plan your meet the teacher open house night.* Young Teacher Love. https://youngteacherlove.com/meet-the-teacher-open-house-night-editable-template/

Nowak, Claire. (2020, March 19). *The 34 most inspirational quotes about teaching.* Reader's Digest. https://www.rd.com/list/teaching-quotes/

1stopteachershop. (2019, February 19). *10 time management tips for teachers.* One Stop Teacher Shop. https://onestopteachershop.com/2019/02/time-management-tips_teachers.html

Pedler, M. (2019, June 6). *Teachers play a key role in helping students feel they "belong" at school.* The Conversation. https://theconversation.com/teachers-play-a-key-role-in-helping-students-feel-they-belong-at-school-99641

Porges, S. (2016, November 28). *The science of breathing: How slowing it down can make us calm and productive.* Forbes.

https://www.forbes.com/sites/sethporges/2016/11/28/the-science-of-breathing-how-slowing-it-down-makes-us-calm-and-productive/#97eb9aa4034e

Resilient Educator Editorial Team. (2013, January 11). *5 Time management tips for teachers*. Resilient Educator. https://resilienteducator.com/classroom-resources/five-time-management-tips-for-teachers/

Schreiber, A. (2018, September 19). *24 reasons children act out—and how to respond*. Motherly. https://www.mother.ly/child/24-reasons-children-act-outand-how-to-respond/theyre-tired

Shalaway, L. (2019). *25 Sure-fire strategies for handling difficult students*. Scholastic.Com. https://www.scholastic.com/teachers/articles/teaching-content/25-sure-fire-strategies-handling-difficult-students/

Sinead Hamill. (2015, August 5). *The effects of labelling children*. MummyPages. https://www.mummypages.ie/the-effects-of-labelling-children

Stutman, M. (2016, January 9). *Listen up! Inspiring quotes for kids about listening*. InspireMyKids. https://inspiremykids.com/2016/listen-up-inspiring-quotes-for-kids-about-listening/#:~:text=Now%2C%20here%20are%20some%20great%20quotes%20for%20kids

Tapp, F. (2020, February 26). *Teacher burnout: Causes, symptoms, and prevention.* Hey Teach! https://www.wgu.edu/heyteach/article/teacher-burnout-causes-symptoms-and-prevention1711.html#:~:text=%20Signs%20of%20Burnout%20%201%20Fatigue%20and

Taylor, J. (2020, April 27). *How to maximize creativity when teaching online.* The Art of Education University. https://theartofeducation.edu/2020/04/27/how-to-maximize-creativity-when-teaching-online/

Terada, Y. (2018, October 24). *Dos and don'ts of classroom decorations.* Edutopia. https://www.edutopia.org/article/dos-and-donts-classroom-decorations

TFA Editorial Team. (2016, October 16). *10 ways to secure your students' attention.* TeachForAmerica.Org. https://www.teachforamerica.org/stories/10-ways-to-secure-your-students-attention

TFA Editorial Team. (2020, March 24). *7 Tips for being a great virtual teacher.* TeachForAmerica.Org. https://www.teachforamerica.org/stories/7-tips-for-being-a-great-virtual-teacher

The 7 best ways to keep students' attention in class. (n.d.). Wabisabi Learning. https://wabisabilearning.com/blogs/inquiry/7-ways-keep-students-attention

Tracy, B. (2019, September 6). *Importance of goal setting: 6 reasons to take setting goals seriously.* Brian Tracy International. https://www.briantracy.com/blog/personal-success/importance-of-goal-setting/

Travis, A. (2020, July). *Teachers are creating incredible bitmoji classrooms for their students.* Distractify. https://www.distractify.com/p/how-to-create-a-bitmoji-classroom

Young, S. C. (2017). *The art of being: 8 ways to optimize your presence & essence for positive impact (The art of first impressions for positive impact)* (Vol. 1). ReNew You Ventures.

Yuan, X., & Che, L. (2012). How to deal with student misbehaviour in the classroom? *Journal of Educational and Developmental Psychology*, 2(1). https://doi.org/10.5539/jedp.v2n1p143